50 YEARS OF

EMMERDALE

First published in Great Britain in 2022 by Cassell, an imprint of
Octopus Publishing Group Ltd
Carmelite House
50 Victoria Embankment
London EC4Y 0DZ
www.octopusbooks.co.uk

An Hachette UK Company
www.hachette.co.uk

Distributed in the US by Hachette Book Group
1290 Avenue of the Americas
4th and 5th Floors, New York, NY 10104

Distributed in Canada by Canadian Manda Group
664 Annette Street, Toronto, Ontario, Canada M6S 2C8

ISBN 978-1-78840-316-0

A CIP catalogue record for this book is available from the British Library.

Printed and bound in China

10 9 8 7 6 5 4 3 2 1

Publisher: Trevor Davies
Art Director: Juliette Norsworthy
Senior Editor: Pauline Bache
Deputy Picture Research Manager: Jennifer Veall
Designer: Rachel Cross
Copyeditor: Helena Caldon
Production Controller: Serena Savini
ITV Head of Publishing: Shirley Patton

Commissioned illustrations for Octopus Publishing Group by Jeff Parker
Commissioned photography for Octopus Publishing Group by Richard Clatworthy

All programme still and cast photos courtesy ITV/Shutterstock with the exception of the following:
ITV: 9, 21 above, 150 below, 197, 198 below, 209, 219, 228 below, 253 below. Jessica Taylor: 243 above
left. Courtesy of the Kevin Laffan Estate: 14. Paul D: 255 above & below. Sandra von Zeist: 243 below.
Shutterstock: 173 below; Anthony Harvey 228 centre; Chris McHugh 136 below left; Jeff Morris/ANL 18 left.
Tom Parfitt: 125 below. Gatefold map: © Katherine Baxter.

EMMERDALE

50 EST. 1972

50 YEARS OF

EMMERDALE

The official story of TV's most iconic rural drama

Tom Parfitt

itv STUDIOS

C CASSELL

CONTENTS

PREFACE

'Ay, it's grand here, in't it.'
Betty Eagleton

Laugh, cry, identify, entertain, inform: that is why people watch *Emmerdale*, but for those involved in making the show, both in front of and behind the camera. The two things that connect them all are the dedication of every single person involved in making the show possible, and the deep affection that drives each cog in the huge machine that is *Emmerdale*.

From those involved in the early days...

FRAZER HINES (Joe Sugden)
'An audience gets used to something. You could have two people talking in the pub, two talking heads, and people will watch. I think it'll go on for another 50 years.'

Frazer Hines behind a camera

FREDDIE PYNE (Matt Skilbeck)
'The company was a good company to work for, and the company of actors were very, very lovely to work with. It was hard work but very easygoing at the same time. I went to visit my brother in New Zealand at one time and when I got on the plane to leave, suddenly over the speakers, came the theme tune. I never asked, I never knew how that happened.'

PAUL LAFFAN (son of *Emmerdale* creator, Kevin Laffan)
'It's been nice thinking about Dad and what he did. My sense from the people I met at Yorkshire Television and the actors, was that there was a great deal of respect for him.'

JEAN ROGERS (Dolly Skilbeck)
'One of the last things my mum said was how important *Emmerdale* was for her – struggling with her illness, *Emmerdale* took her mind away, with the lovely Yorkshire setting. It's a privilege to be an actor and be a character that people want in their homes every day.'

MALANDRA BURROWS (Kathy Glover)
'I don't know what life would have been without it. It certainly grounded me, made me the person I am, my love of animals, and the countryside, that definitely stayed with me. I've never got married, but then again, looking at my *Emmerdale* history I can kind of see why! I still feel so involved, there's people who I meet to this day who stop and want to talk about it and want to know about it.'

To those long-running actors...

CHRIS CHITTELL (Eric Pollard)

'Our wonderful cast, crew and production are as one; the humour, the banter, the care and commitment are integral to our success as a programme.'

CLAIRE KING (Kim Tate)

'It's still got the best work ethic and it's still the most down to earth place, and I know people always say 'oh it's like a family' but it really is. I think it's also because we're the only one that has the greenery, the rural setting, the beautiful Dales, it just looks different from city soaps. And there's such a variety of different people because of the setting: there are people from the city, there are country bumpkins and you wouldn't normally get that on a soap. It lends itself to having all these diverse characters in there, which is great.'

JAMES HOOTON (Sam Dingle)

'It's a life-changing experience to work with such a good ensemble team. There are still people involved in the show that I was with on the first day, there are no airs and graces, no one's above anyone else – it's the best formula for getting the job done.'

LISA RILEY (Mandy Dingle)

'The root of *Emmerdale* is brilliant families, like a crochet blanket. We've had these family-driven characters for so long, and viewers care – they want to know what they're doing, because we're in their household night after night. That's what makes it so terrific. I honestly feel like I'm part of the heart of the programme, and that fills me with pride.'

MARK CHARNOCK (Marlon Dingle)

'It's been a gift, all the way through. I can honestly say, 25 years later, I genuinely get excited to go in every day. It's a support network, it's a hot bed of creativity. I used to watch it when I was a little boy, with my grandparents. It's a little piece of magic in the world.'

SAMANTHA GILES (Bernice Blackstock)

'It's had an enormous impact on my life. I think there's a tendency for people to be dismissive of soaps, but they are a huge part of many people's lives. I feel very lucky that I've played a character that has been very popular.'

Claire King as Kim Tate

TONY AUDENSHAW (Bob Hope)

'It's a factory for making TV that people engage with. It's a great job for me because I can do what I enjoy, I can do serious stuff, I can do a bit of comedy, I can sing a bit. It plays to my strengths as an actor, and I feel valued there. It's not about giving people what they want all the time, so we're not just making the audience happy, we're annoying them, you want to keep them watching and you want to take them on a journey. Characters are taken out of their comfort zones and do something bad and go on a curve of redemption.'

Lisa Riley as Mandy Dingle

NICOLA WHEELER (Nicola King)
'It tells stories that we've all been through, and it gives audience members hope or makes them feel like they're not alone. I've experienced poverty in my 20s, so hand on heart I feel grateful, because I know what it's like to live on the other side, where you live in a flat full of fleas and you can't afford to heat your home. *Emmerdale*'s kept me doing what I do, so I'm eternally grateful – it's been a big part of my life'

LUCY PARGETER (Chas Dingle)
'I absolutely love that place with all my heart. I look forward to going to work every day. I love the people I work with, across the board. It's like reality TV but watching the same people growing up over the years. And it's a routine and people like that, especially during lockdown. They come home, have their tea and watch their soaps.'

CHARLOTTE BELLAMY (Laurel Thomas)
'It's kind of shaped me as a person. I became a mother when my character became a mother, as the show's evolved, so have I. I owe everything to the show. It's the best place to work, it's an honour to be there, every day I'm grateful. The village is magical.'

From those who have grown up on-screen...

EDEN TAYLOR-DRAPER (Belle Dingle)
'I genuinely love the show: within half an hour you're seeing ten different real stories that affect people. I can't imagine what I'd be like if I hadn't grown up on there. Everyone I've grown up with has added into my personality and the way I am.'

JOE-WARREN PLANT (Jacob Gallagher)
'It's really helped me, being around adults my whole life, it's benefited me with social skills, so I'm really thankful to have been given an opportunity like this. To grow up with such generous people, I can't even explain how proud I aim to be part of *Emmerdale*.'

Jurell Carter as Nate Robinson

And the more recent additions...

CHRIS BISSON (Jai Sharma)
'Every single person who comes through this building has a job to do, and if any of those parts fail, the whole machine tends to grind to a halt. Working on the village set is a joy. There is something special, and there's a real privilege that you are reminded of on those spring mornings when you're driving to the village and you think "this is where I work".'

MICHELLE HARDWICK (Vanessa Woodfield)
'I watched *Emmerdale* as a child with my grandparents, so it means a great deal personally that I'm working on a show that I grew up with!'

JURELL CARTER (Nate Robinson)
'To be a part of such a massive show is amazing. I'm learning every single day and I think being around genuinely nice and talented people, cast and crew, is a blessing. It was my late grandma's favourite show, and my parents' favourite show, and it means everything that they're proud of me.'

To those behind the scenes...

DUNCAN FOSTER (Director)

'*Emmerdale*'s one of the nicest places to work, with great cast and crew, who are just as enthusiastic as you about making the best programme we can. I've always said, I'll always come and direct *Emmerdale*, whatever I'm doing in my career, because it's such a fabulous place to work and I'd miss it. Who wouldn't want to go out and film in that village. It's the best set, by a million miles, it's a massive blank canvas; it's got everything that you need.'

KATE BROOKS (Producer)

'I've always been a fan of *Emmerdale*, and I've always been in awe of how it pushes boundaries and can tell stories in non-linear ways – which to me keeps the genre of soap fresh and exciting. So it has been a real privilege to play a small part in making 50 years' worth of brilliant drama.'

JANE HUDSON (Executive Producer)

'I'm incredibly proud of being from Yorkshire, it was the soap I grew up on. The only reason I learned to play the oboe, to grade eight standard, was because the original *Emmerdale* theme tune was played on the oboe. *Emmerdale* means so much to me because of who I am and where I come from.'

LAURA SHAW (Producer)

'I love the show to bits, from watching as a child to working on it now. To be involved in a show that's been on for 50 years, watched by millions, just feels incredible, and I feel so grateful that they've let me work here for so long.'

NADER MABADI (Head of Production)

'My partner works in critical care, and we were at a doctors' ball. I felt like an imposter in the room, surrounded by surgeons, doctors and nurses. I got talking to a surgeon and told him what I did, embarrassed in comparison. He said, "What do you think we have in every ward, next to every bed? Televisions. People, when they're going through trouble, or pain, the one thing that we have in life, is a box that can project people who are maybe going through something similar, or for you to escape from what's going on in their own world. It might entertain, or educate, or inform, or relate. You are providing something that, to millions of people every day, holds people together. *Emmerdale* to me, is an opportunity to be socially responsible and allows me to connect with people in a way that I'm so privileged to do. That responsibility for me is something I treasure.'

Producers Laura Shaw, Jane Hudson and Kate Brooks

INTRODUCTION

AT 1:30PM ON 16 OCTOBER 1972, a new twice-weekly farming serial first broadcast on Yorkshire Television. Aimed at housewives, in a new daytime TV slot, the original 26-episode run told the saga of three generations of the hearty, down-to-earth Sugden family and their home, Emmerdale Farm. In that moment, no one could have foreseen that this genteel, picturesque slice of rural life would, five decades later, be a six-episodes-a-week, award-winning, internationally broadcast powerhouse of storytelling about a fictional Yorkshire Dales village. This isn't one street, one square, one cul-de-sac; what started out as one farm now encapsulates life in a whole village; a rural community of all walks of life: from those struggling to make a living off the land, to those lording it over everyone with their spoils up at the manor.

Emmerdale's story is unique. The show's road to success and recognition is a journey of adapting, evolving and surviving. A journey of building on its solid farming roots established by creator Kevin Laffan, gaining affection in the nation's hearts, and seizing its rightful place as one of Britain's longest-running, highest-rated and best-loved continuing dramas. Everything has got bigger across the soap's history: the output, the set, the cast, the stunts, the stronger and more ambitious storytelling, and the awards, recognition and impact on its audience. The ultimate guide to decades of entertainment, this book breaks down the DNA of the Dales. How did a sleepy bi-weekly serial about one farm survive for 50 years? Within these chapters, the show's journey from its humble beginning, through to its solid status as one of Britain's most popular dramas, is mapped out. The escapism of the aspirational, beautiful village setting is showcased. The generations of family, of unique and recognizable characters, is explored. The rivalry, secrets, humour and scandal that interweave through the show's history of contemporary stories are remembered. The constantly evolving pace and scale of production is celebrated.

This is a tribute to all those who have been involved – from cast and crew, to the loyal fanbase the show continues to enjoy, old and new, who are rewarded with a unique window into a remarkable piece of television history.

'I think *Emmerdale* is on fire at the minute, because we've got a fantastic mix of characters; we've got characters who've been in the show for decades, and we've got some wonderful new talent with us. We've got a fantastic mix of diversity, we've got more people of colour in *Emmerdale* than we've ever had, which was absolutely one of my main incentives when I came here: to improve diversity on-screen. I think we have a fantastic mix of stories, which are really sad and emotional, and other stories that are comical and make you laugh. We do the best stunts of any drama on television! We manage to hit a really good balance of being entertaining and also being thought-provoking. I know that sometimes it's hard to express how you're feeling, sometimes you feel you shouldn't cry, for example, but when you see a character on your television six times a week, who you might see more often than your own family, and you see them crying over a death, it almost provides you with an outlet to do it, the same place for you to do that with your emotions. We keep that connection between character and viewer.'

Jane Hudson *(Executive Producer)*

CHAPTER 1

CONCEPT & EVOLUTION

'There's virtually no relation to the show that Kevin Laffan created now – it's evolved, but it's done it some good. It's completely to our advantage.'
Bill Lyons *(Writer)*

Soaps are never averse to change – being moved about the schedule, having multiple episodes a night, or more episodes per week – but *Emmerdale* is on another level. From the beginning, it's been about change and evolution, both on- and off-screen. The death of Jacob Sugden and the carving up of the family farm into a business involving several family generations – as well as wealthy outsiders – set the tone for the next 50 years. By the time *Emmerdale* had firmly evolved into a soap opera, during the mid-90s, *EastEnders* and *Coronation Street* were vying for top ratings and awards, but as *Emmerdale*'s storytelling, character base and popularity went from strength to strength, the two-horse race was over. *Emmerdale*'s position was cemented, and the show was here to stay.

KEVIN LAFFAN:
Planting the Emmerdale seed

'I think he was happier when it was just him and his typewriter!'

Mike Laffan (*son of Kevin Laffan*)

AS ONE OF a family of 14 children living in poverty, Kevin Laffan would have had no idea that in the decades to come he'd create something that would capture television audiences for 50 years and counting. Born in 1922, Kevin was a young teenager when his family were so poor, they were taken to the workhouse. 'He jumped off the back of the wagon, and ran away,' Kevin's son, Mike, explains. 'He did various jobs: gardener's boy, farmer's boy, delivery boy, then he joined the Birmingham Old Vic.' Early family life with his wife Jeanne – who he would be married to for over 50 years – and their three sons, Mike, Dave and Paul, was filled with Kevin's working life in theatre. 'We used to go down to Ilfracombe, where my parents ran a theatre during the summer, and prior to that, he ran a theatre in Reading,' Mike recalls, 'Around the time I

was born, television was coming in and he started to do small acting jobs, and then he started writing.'

'He worked on a lot of long-running series, rather than serials, so he'd drive off to Leeds, to spend a bit of time away. He clocked up a lot of miles in those years,' Mike recalls. 'He used to write for programmes like *Man and a Suitcase*, which was a spy thing. He'd done a soap called *Castle Haven*, which was set in a seaside town, then he was asked to do *Emmerdale*.'

'Dad wanted to keep the locations looking pretty rudimentary, while the production team wanted to warm them up and make them look more affluent,' Paul explains. 'He grasped that making life a little bit more gentle gave the series a very human warmth, and that made the series very attractive to viewers.'

Kevin wrote for *Emmerdale* until 1985, while working on other projects and gaining further success with sitcoms, *Beryl's Lot* and *I Thought You'd Gone*. 'He was pretty systematic as a writer,' Mike recalls. 'When it was too noisy, he'd go out, he'd sit in churchyards and things like that. He had a theatrical feel for what captured people's interests, and what caused friction.'

Kevin passed away in 2003, aged 80. 'I think he always felt proud of *Emmerdale*,' Mike muses. 'He started it from scratch, and saw it through into mainstream schedule, but eventually it wasn't what he created. I think he was happier when it was just him and his typewriter.'

'We were a bi-weekly serial that had a break in the middle of the year. We're a walk in the country, with animals, for those that are stuck in their houses, or stuck on the dole, or stuck in nine-to-five jobs.'

Ian Sharrock (*Jackie Merrick*)

The first episode netted two million viewers, and in response to the audience enjoying the breath of country air, *Emmerdale Farm* was extended to 26 weeks – 52 episodes. 'One of our PAs came up to us as we were having lunch in the canteen, and out of the corner of her mouth said, "I've just seen the scripts for episode 27",' Frazer Hines recalls. 'So we had another six months' work. The six months became a year. Then we had a year's contract.'

'After the first year I went to the script editors and asked, "Do you think it's going to run?", as I was still paying rent and I wanted to buy a house,' Freddie Pyne explains. 'So I put a deposit on a house, a semi. Never did I think it was going to go on for so long. I thought I'd stay five years, but you get hooked into these things!' The drama series continued to grow, still at two episodes a week, and taking a pause in the summer months. It would be 1988 before

The original cast outside Emmerdale Farm

the programme received a simultaneous network transmission, and 1990 before it moved to a prime-time network 7pm evening slot. 'It was very tied into the farming year. There was a farmer, and Dad used to get a synopsis from the farmer about what they were doing – mowed the meadow, brought the sheep out, that sort of thing, and he really liked that,' Mike recalls.

'Dad understood that part of the appeal of *Emmerdale* was a certain amount of rural escapism, it used to be advertised on the tube as "Country Breaks, Twice a Week",' Kevin's son Paul explains. 'However, he wanted there to be a level of realism. The farm kitchen's fourth wall had the sink up against it. When Matt and Joe came in, it was usually for meals, and the first thing they did was walk up to the sink and wash their hands – very important for a farmer before eating. People actually commented to me about how much they liked the characters doing this.'

'Kevin had said he wanted it to be like a Dickens novel – a year or so and then finish,' Freddie Pyne recalls. 'And here we are 50 years later and it's still going!'

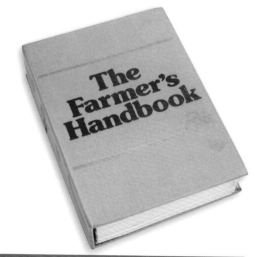
An indispensable guide to country living for early scriptwriters

EVOLUTION OF FILMING & SETTING

'When we first had the village, the bridle path across the top is a public right of way and often you'd see walkers with backpacks and sticks stopping and looking, because the village is not on their map, and then they'd realize what's down there.'
John Middleton *(Ashley Thomas)*

WHEN *EMMERDALE FARM* began filming in 1972, Lindley Farm, near Harrogate, was used for the exteriors of Emmerdale Farm, while anything filmed in the fictitious Beckindale village was, in reality, the village of Arncliffe, in the Yorkshire Dales. In the show's early years, with an abundance of farm scenes to shoot, some cast members had a taller order than others. 'Frazer and I had a hell of a lot of work to do; we had cows to milk and sheep to shear,' Freddie Pyne recalls. 'We had to be in the studios by 6am for makeup, then like an hour and a half drive to Arncliffe or Lindley.' Interior scenes, from the show's conception through to 1989, were filmed in Yorkshire Television's Leeds Studios, on Kirkstall Road.

From 1976, exterior village filming moved to the village of Esholt, which was closer to the Yorkshire Television Studios, meaning less time transporting cast and crew. The local village hall in Esholt was used as a production base, for costume, makeup, props and as a green room. The village pub, The Commercial Inn, was used for The Woolpack exteriors, with a temporary Woolpack sign added whenever filming took place. Eventually, the pub officially changed its name to The Woolpack. While the location of Esholt was not revealed officially, it didn't take viewers long to work it out and soon tourists flocked to see their favourite TV village. 'Bus companies used to bus in tourists, but that caused problems,' former production controller Tim Fee remembers. 'There was a guy who lived there that the crew called The Lawnmower Man, because whenever we started filming, he'd start up his lawnmower. One day I knocked on his door to find out what the problem was, and in his sitting room there was a rumbling, and all the plaster on the walls was cracked – the coaches were parking alongside his wall. I got rid of the coaches, and in four weeks we were friends.'

Arncliffe, the original village set

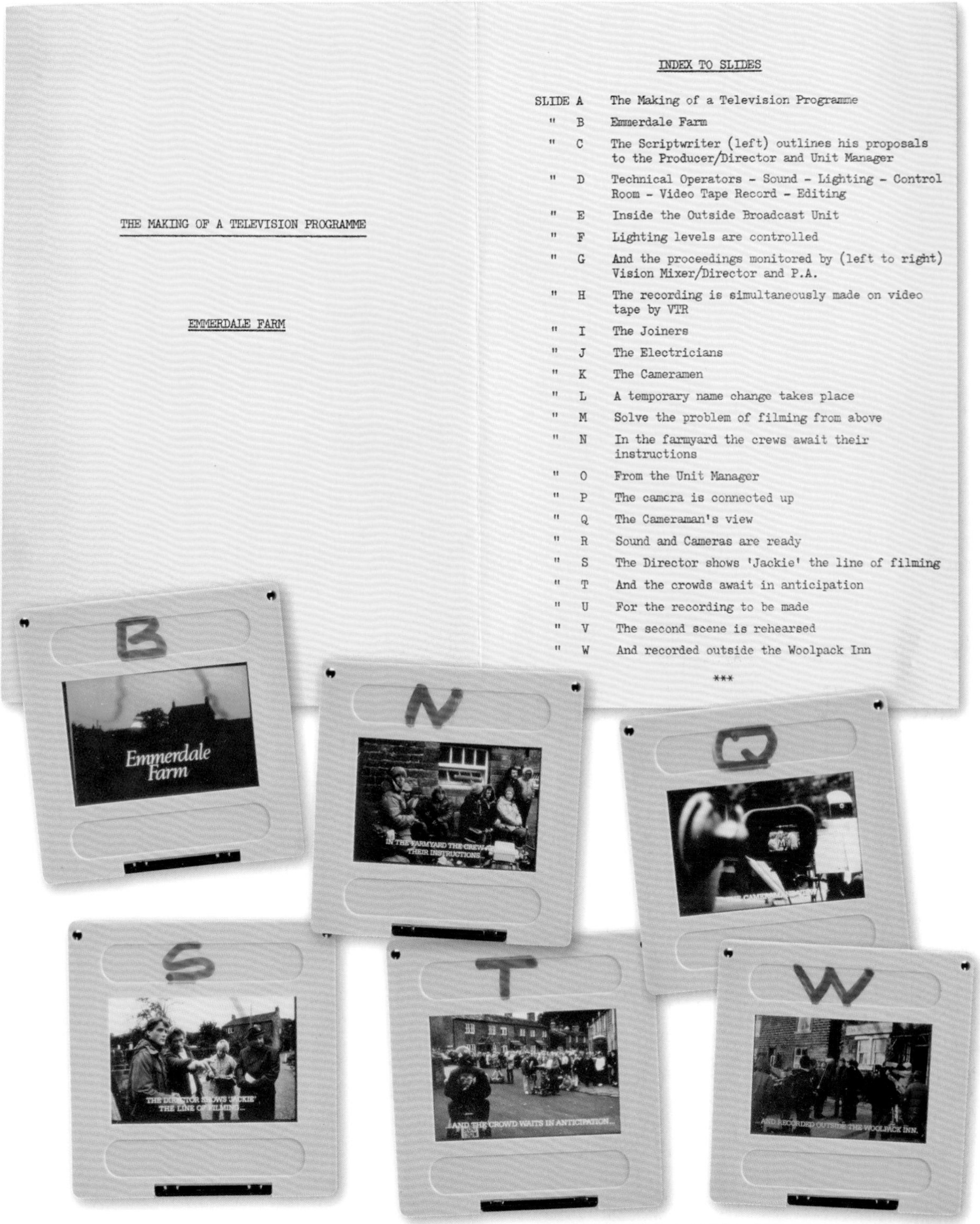

THE MAKING OF A TELEVISION PROGRAMME

EMMERDALE FARM

INDEX TO SLIDES

SLIDE	A	The Making of a Television Programme
"	B	Emmerdale Farm
"	C	The Scriptwriter (left) outlines his proposals to the Producer/Director and Unit Manager
"	D	Technical Operators – Sound – Lighting – Control Room – Video Tape Record – Editing
"	E	Inside the Outside Broadcast Unit
"	F	Lighting levels are controlled
"	G	And the proceedings monitored by (left to right) Vision Mixer/Director and P.A.
"	H	The recording is simultaneously made on video tape by VTR
"	I	The Joiners
"	J	The Electricians
"	K	The Cameramen
"	L	A temporary name change takes place
"	M	Solve the problem of filming from above
"	N	In the farmyard the crews await their instructions
"	O	From the Unit Manager
"	P	The camera is connected up
"	Q	The Cameraman's view
"	R	Sound and Cameras are ready
"	S	The Director shows 'Jackie' the line of filming
"	T	And the crowds await in anticipation
"	U	For the recording to be made
"	V	The second scene is rehearsed
"	W	And recorded outside the Woolpack Inn

***

Slides and index to show 'The Making of a Television Programme'

The Commercial Inn, Esholt

The Woolpack today

When production controller Tim Fee first took on the role, he was tasked with finding a new production centre and studios for the then bi-weekly series. 'I came across a little wool mill in Farsley. It was a four-storey building that was completely unused. So that's where the home for *Emmerdale* came from – the studio, the offices, costume, makeup, rehearsals, everything.' Deena Payne remembers working at Farsley. 'Monday and Tuesday were rehearsals, Wednesday was the producer's run and Thursday/ Friday it was Kathy's Tearoom or The Woolpack,' Deena explains. 'The following week was Sugdens' or anything outside. So you could read the scripts because it was four; two each week, and if you had no outside stuff, you'd only work one of the weeks!' But not all the cast were fans of the Farsley Mill setup. 'We had four floors, and to get up, an old lift with a metal zigzag grill thing that you pulled open,' Tim recalls. 'Sheila Mercier once got in the lift and it stopped between floors and she was stuck, and we had to get the lift people to get her out. Sheila said she would never go in that lift again, unless I was with her!'

As *Emmerdale*'s production continued to expand throughout the 1990s, moving from two to three episodes a week, the decision was made to return production to Leeds, to a dedicated space not far from the original studios. 'Burley Road was known as the OB garage (Outside Broadcast garage),' Tim explains. 'We had to lay studio floors, and that was the world's largest television studio. We laid a wooden floor, which was a disaster, because it did nothing but creak!' *Emmerdale*'s new production centre was officially opened by the prime minister, John Major, on 6 January 1997, and boasted studio space of 24,000 square feet.

Production moved back to the Yorkshire Television Studios in nearby Kirkstall Road in 2010, when the studios were upgraded to HD standard. The former Burley Road buildings, as well as still being used for sets such as the hospital, police station and Home Farm, housed the *Emmerdale* Experience Tour, a popular visitor attraction.

At Esholt, the increase in production output was causing more disruption and congestion than ever to the village, and Executive Producer Keith Richardson became increasingly aware of the need for a purpose-built closed set dedicated to *Emmerdale*. 'Keith told me to find somewhere to build a village!' Tim laughs. 'At that time we'd introduced the Dingles and we used to shoot at the farm at Harewood, and I was looking out across the land. I knew those fields would be ideal: the land was boggy, so no good for farmers, so I suspected that we could do a deal!'

A 300-acre site was leased, with planning permission granted in June 1997 to build a village set. As the structures were built on green-belt land, the planning needs renewing every ten years, and should *Emmerdale* ever cease to use the site, it has to be returned to exactly as it was before. After strict consultation with conservation organizations, building work began on the multi-million-pound project – with plans for a church and vicarage pulled to save money. A team of over 100 builders worked constantly over 20 weeks to complete the village by the end of 1997. The village itself takes up around 11 acres of land, and has its own electricity and water supply, as well as drainage, phone and internet, and a security system. Five hundred tons of crushed limestone was used to create a mile-long access road to the main road.

Then 28 timber-framed structures were erected and clad in Yorkshire stone, with the designers and builders using several tricks of the trade to age the

buildings and make them look authentic. Roofs were built to sag, the structures were sandblasted to add distress, and the walls sprayed with a yoghurt and manure mixture to encourage lichen to grow quickly – all to give the appearance of a village that was 500 years old. Each of the cottages has a chimney fitted with a smoke machine, which is controlled by a switch. Half a mile of drystone walling was added, as well as 900 square miles of turf.

While many of the interiors are filmed in the studios, some are filmed in the actual buildings at Harewood, including Pollard's Barn, Holdgate Farm, Smithy Cottage, the vet's surgery, Brook Cottage, the B&B, the garage, the village hall, the cricket pavilion, Farrers Barn, Connelton View and the church. All of the upstairs rooms in the village buildings are used as bedrooms, redressed for whatever the needs of the story or script are.

The remaining buildings at Harewood have a secondary production purpose inside:

Wishing Well Cottage: *Christmas prop store*
HOP: *bikes store*
Tall Trees Cottage: *Abbott Lane Surgery set*
Mulberry Cottage: *prop store*
The Woolpack: *food prep and part replica of studio set*
Pear Tree Cottage: *costume*
Woodbine Cottage: *makeup*
Tug Ghyll: *toilets and security*
Dale Head: *green room and admin*
Mill Cottage: *silk flower and plant store*
David's Shop: *store*
Tenant House and Jacobs Fold: *monitor rooms*
Dale View: *waiting area for extras*
Victoria Cottage: *crew tearoom*
Keepers Cottage: *grips storage*
Café Main Street: *monitor room*

EVOLUTION OF CHARACTERS

'The same as the other soaps, it's representing aspects of life that people can identify with, and in *Emmerdale* especially, you have the underclass Dingles, and you've got the big house on the hill with the Tates, who people might aspire to be like.'
James Hooton (*Sam Dingle*)

WITH A PICTURESQUE setting, *Emmerdale* has always needed myriad inhabitants to enable the village story mill to grind away and to keep millions tuning in every night. With a whole community of people whose lives are on show, there's a full complement of characters from all walks of life.

The Sugdens, typical 'farming folk' of the Dales

Although the show initially revolved principally around Emmerdale Farm and the Sugden family, who represented the 'farming folk' of the Dales, viewers also got a window into the lives of the parish vicar, the pub landlords, the landed gentry at the manor and the prosperous mill owner. While stories of Emmerdale Farm were the bread and butter of the show for the first two decades, viewers began to see content that enveloped the wider community. 'My character, Dolly, was running the playgroup, and occasionally worked in The Woolpack, so the show was moving into the village,' explains Jean Rogers. By the close of the 1980s, the word 'Farm' had been dropped from the title, as the programme now merged into soap opera, and stories centring on other areas and families of the village now began to overtake those from the Sugdens and their farm. 'Because it got more successful, it couldn't keep just revolving round the farm,' Frazer Hines explains. 'You had to, like an octopus, grow another tentacle and another tentacle, it had to reach out further into the village.'

With the wider village setting being the key to discovering new characters and easing the strain on the Sugdens for stories, more emphasis was placed on Home Farm by the end of the 1980s, and so a proper established family was brought in: the Tates.

The Bartons revamped the image of farming for the 21st century

'I think you got that sense that it was the end of an old era and the start of a new, and I think that was the intention of actually bringing in the Tate family,' Claire King recalls. 'They were this flash, nouveau-riche family and you could see it was going to go in a different direction.'

As the floodgates opened to a wider range of characters, more 'non-Yorkshire folk' moved up from down south, with the introduction in 1993 of the Windsor and McAllister families. Deena Payne recalls her audition for Viv Windsor. 'I did the worst accent. I'd bumped into a friend on the Underground, and she said "go with the accent", so I went in with this awful Cockney accent, and once I'd started I couldn't stop. When I did a screen test, I lost a bit of the accent!' By 1994, in contrast to the Tates and the more well-to-do villagers, the Dingle family had emerged. This proved to be one of the show's greatest moves, as that family unit alone would provide diversity in generation, disability, race, sexuality and social mobility for decades to come.

The 1990s and 2000s saw an influx of younger characters, to help focus stories on contemporary issues affecting the next generation, but *Emmerdale* was careful to retain its legendary senior members.

'Edna and Betty are quintessentially the essence of what villages used to be,' Nicola Wheeler explains. 'Those characters were the best and the worst of people – the gossips, but they were kind and generous to others. Yes, they were judgemental but at the same time they'd take anyone into their homes. They're the essence of what a neighbour is.'

As Clive Hornby's passing marked an end to the original Sugden dynasty, *Emmerdale* injected a new farm family in 2009, billed as 'Farming Gets Sexy', with the Bartons; and the Sharma family, also introduced in 2009, became the first Asian family for *Emmerdale*. Chris Bisson recalls his hopes. 'I was keen that there wasn't a lot of reference to their ethnicity because I didn't want it to be "the Asian family". I think we're past that now, and we wanted to play run-of-the-mill stories. The sooner race doesn't become an issue, or it's never even considered anymore, we're in a better place as a society.'

Emmerdale now paints its stories from a broader palette of characters than ever before, reflecting the contemporary society we live in, promoting equality and giving voice to as many different groups as possible – whether through gay, lesbian, bisexual or asexual characters, trans characters, disabled characters or ethnic minorities.

Ethan Anderson speaks out for equality and acceptance at Pride

EVOLUTION OF STORIES

'You can have a much more dynamic number of stories, because it's across class and you can have class clashes and that makes it very interesting. It means a lot more people can identify with it.'
John Middleton (*Ashley Thomas*)

WHAT STARTED OUT as a genteel, twice-weekly drama about one farm is now a hotbed of innovative, often groundbreaking storytelling, giving viewers a piece of 21st-century village life six times a week. To fulfil that quota, and remain appealing to a contemporary audience, *Emmerdale* has adapted, turning from a trusty, manual plough, through to a high-performance machine, forging its own furrow with modern storylines.

It's never been easier to switch channel, so keeping viewers hooked is paramount. The ways in which *Emmerdale* tells stories continue to evolve, with the show employing flashbacks, flashforwards, two-handers, whodunnits and single-perspective episodes. With stories ranging from Sam Pearson's factitious upholding of the Beating of the Bounds tradition, to drag artist The Vivienne's appearance at Emmerdale's first Pride event, *Emmerdale* consistently delivers storylines both topical and entertaining.

A common misconception of the early years was of a sleepy rural serial in which little happened. But in the first few years there was a brutal rape and murder, several other sexual attacks and sudden deaths – including the tragic killing of twin toddlers – high-octane stories were prevalent from the off.

While tales of farm life remained the show's bread and butter for the first few decades, the programme's focus gradually shifted beyond the gate of Emmerdale Farm and into the wider village. By the time of one of the show's biggest turning points, the 1993 plane crash, every character in the village was now drawn into the ensemble story that helped elevate *Emmerdale*'s profile. 'We were always considered a lower pedestal than *EastEnders* and *Corrie*,' explains Claire King. 'So as much as people thought this is going to be OTT, it really did save *Emmerdale*'s bacon.'

Emmerdale was now firmly a soap opera. The farm remained an important asset of its makeup, but there was a definitive switch to stories from all walks of village life – from the community rallying around the outcast Dingle family, through to the bedhopping and boardroom backstabbing of the Tates.

The age-old village tradition, beating of the bounds, in 1974

The community protests the attempted eviction of the Dingles in 1995

Coverage of village events has evolved from the Silver Jubilee and Boxing Day hunts of the 1970s and 1980s to protest groups fighting against Nuclear Waste Dumping and Foxhunting in the 1980s and 1990s, and stories addressing issues of equality in the 2000s and 2010s. Aside from these political plotlines, *Emmerdale* continues to adapt its personal stories to reflect the contemporary world; whether through the controversial new farming methods of Alan Turner, which clashed with the traditional Sugdens in the early 1980s, or more recently in addressing racial prejudice, with black characters Ethan and Charles Anderson in the early 2020s. During the late 70s and early 80s, there were prevalent miscarriage and stillbirth stories with Dolly Skilbeck, and teenage pregnancy, abortion and adoption issues explored with Sandie Merrick, and by the dawn of the 90s, *Emmerdale* had a male single parent: Nick Bates.

Throughout the 2000s and 2010s *Emmerdale*'s issue-led content won praise, through stories of Laurel and Ashley's cot death tragedy, Zak and Belle Dingle's mental health struggles, Ashley's dementia and Aaron's struggle to come out, garnered praise for tackling tough but important subject matter. 'We were starting to be taken really seriously with Aaron's gay self-loathing story,' explains writer Karin Young. 'That changed people's perception of the show and we won awards we'd never really won before.'

Emmerdale's first Pride event, in 2021

CHAPTER 2

THE SETTINGS

'The real star of *Emmerdale* is the village. It's very evocative as a backdrop, and whatever drama's happening, you've got the sound of sheep and tractors, and a rural village pub. It's just a very pleasant thing to watch...apart from when there's a disaster!'

Charlotte Bellamy *(Laurel Thomas)*

The heart of any soap is its setting, and there's none more picturesque than the idyllic rural backdrop of Emmerdale – the ultimate viewer escapism. Originally called Beckindale, then renamed after the plane crash tragedy of 1993, Emmerdale is a small village set in the Yorkshire Dales. In reality, the show's setting has grown from one real-life working farm to the vast acres of the permanent outdoor set on the Harewood Estate, north of Leeds, which has been used since 1998. *Emmerdale*'s sets are among the most recognizable on television, and whether rambling farms, country pubs, quaint cottages or vast manor houses, *Emmerdale* really does have it all.

Emmerdale Farm

The titular Emmerdale Farm is the site of all the action out in the fields as well as the drama within the sprawling aged farmhouse. It has housed several generations and off-shoots of the Sugden clan. The original Emmerdale Farm, used from 1972 to 1993, was filmed on Lindley Farm, in North Yorkshire. The Sugdens had farmed Emmerdale, as tenant farmers, since 1850, and in 1972, Jacob Sugden had been the fourth generation to farm there. 'Joe thought he'd inherit the farm when Jacob died, but Jacob left it to Jack, as the elder son,' Frazer Hines explains. 'Joe resented that Jack had been gallivanting off around the world, writing books, while Joe kept the farm going.' Emmerdale Farm's freehold was purchased by former millowner, Henry Wilks, who suggested forming a limited company with the Sugdens, so that they all had a proper share of the business. Emmerdale Farm Ltd was formed, with Henry, Annie, Jack, and Joe all receiving a share, as well as Annie's father, Sam, and her daughter, Peggy. Sam straight away sold his shares for £500, using the money to buy a new suit.

In 1972, the farm consisted of 320 acres, a mix of sheep, dairy and beef herds, hens and geese, and barley and kale. The farmhouse itself had a front parlour and a large farm kitchen, where most of the family interaction took place. 'We would do all the kitchen scenes in one day,' Frazer Hines recalls. 'We'd turn up for work, Annie's cooking sausage, egg and bacon, then you'd have the lunch scene, a ham salad or something, then we'd have an evening, beef goulash or something. Sometimes you had three meals a day and not have to put your hand in your pocket!' Upstairs in the farm were three bedrooms, with another added in the loft in 1974, when traveller Dryden Hogben, who was camping on Emmerdale land, was tasked with converting it.

'I spent the best part of 50 years in this house. I ran a farm, raised a family and watched my husband die'
Annie Sugden

ACROSS THE 1970S and 80s, several modcons were introduced to the farmhouse, including a telephone, television, washing machine, central heating and a fitted kitchen. An annexe was also converted into a two-bedroom house, in which Jack, Sarah and Robert came to live, with Sarah nailing up the door connecting it to the farmhouse, to stop Annie waltzing in and interfering!

By 1980, with Jack fully immersed in farm life, despondent Joe jumped ship to work for NY Estates, eventually leaving for France for several years. Under Jack's guidance, the farm grew, buying 70 acres of land from Crossgill when Matt and Dolly inherited it. Dolly also ran a small farm shop at Emmerdale, with help from Kathy.

Then 1993 brought Emmerdale's biggest challenge, when Jack's tractor fell into a hole, and doors became difficult to open and close in the house. With the farm suffering from subsidence, Annie was not impressed to return from a holiday in Spain to find her home abandoned, and it took her a long time to come around to the idea of a new farm. Hawthorn Cottage, previously the home of Peggy and Matt, and then Joe and Christine, was acquired to become Emmerdale Farm II, in reality a farm close to Eccup Reservoir.

With an additional 50 acres to add to Emmerdale's existing land, the future looked bright until the 1993 plane crash claimed the life of Joe's stepson, Mark. Struggling with the guilt of sending Mark out to his death (Joe had insisted Mark return a vacuum cleaner to a neighbouring farm on the night), Joe lost interest in the farm, which was ravaged by fuel spillage from the crash. After one too many differences of opinions with Jack, Joe left for Spain, never to return.

By 1995, Joe, Jack and Annie still had shares in the farm, with Annie inheriting Joe's following his death, and promising them to Rachel's baby, Joseph Tate, when he turned 18. Sarah and Jack converted a barn into a bunkhouse for school and corporate trips, but by 1996 Annie wanted to sell, and with pressure from Frank Tate to buy up the farm for an access road to his new quarry, Jack agreed.

Jack and Sarah bought Woodside Farm, but when the place needed more renovation work than they thought, they sold it on to newcomer Tony Cairns for a £50,000 profit – money that enabled them to buy the more expensive Melby Farm. In reality, the new farm was at the entrance to the Harewood site used for the Emmerdale village, and became the third version of Emmerdale Farm, until 2002. With the business having hit the skids once again, Jack finally gave in and sold up – although the Sugdens' tradition of farming would continue the following year, when Andy took the tenancy of Butlers Farm.

The Emmerdale Farm legacy surfaced in 2020, following matriarch Annie Sugden's death, with her parting gift to granddaughter Victoria: a parcel of land that used to form Emmerdale Farm but was now being farmed by Moira at Butlers Farm. Moira panicked over Victoria's plans, but was relieved when Victoria agreed to rent the field to Butlers.

'I feel blessed to have spent my life working on the land, like my dad and his dad before him. When I was out in the fields, I used to feel them there with me. And I'll be there with all of you, in the rain and the snow, when the lambs arrive and when the leaves fall from the trees.'
(Jack Sugden's goodbye letter)

SHOOTING ON REAL-LIFE working farms was not for the faint-hearted, and fortunately *Emmerdale* has been blessed with willing, and skilled, actors who are ready to muck in, quite literally. 'Yorkshire TV were very fortunate to get myself and Freddie Pyne (Matt), two actors who didn't mind getting our hands dirty,' Frazer Hines laughs. 'We hated milking scenes, it was always the end of the day, and you had to know your lines inside and out. You'd put two cows in the stall, and they'd lock their bums together and you couldn't go "Excuse me, the cows have locked their bums together, I can't say my line." You had to know your lines and then ad-lib.'

'I soon learned you keep away from the back end of a cow when you watch the tail swinging!' Jean Rogers adds. 'The biggest challenge was dipping sheep. Every year they have this tank, and each of the sheep are driven through. You have to submerge the sheep in the disinfectant. Freddie (Matt) was driving them in and I was in the middle with the broom, submerging them, and someone else was at the

end, but at the end of that filming day, I was just so exhausted and achy.'

For other members of the cast, it wasn't just the animals that needed careful attention, but the machinery, too. 'We had the scripts written by non-farming folk, so we had a scene where Jackie screams into the farmyard and screeches to a halt in a tractor,' Ian Sharrock recalls. 'So they set the shot up with the camera and cameraman on the floor in the farmyard for the ground shot. But a tractor doesn't stop, it's like a battleship, no matter how hard you brake, you've got five tonnes of steel. We do maybe three takes, and each time, I ended up with my tractor maybe 18 inches from the lens of this camera. None of the crew knew how close they came to being killed. I was driving combine harvesters, tractors and trailers – I can do that as good as any Dales' farmers. There were days when I would have paid them to let me do it.'

Wishing Well Cottage

Chaotic, ramshackle and always on the brink of collapse, the Dingles' infamous homestead is much like its occupants. Originally an outbuilding, Wishing Well has housed over five generations of Dingle since the family first took residence in the 1960s. 'It's open house, anyone's welcomed in with open arms,' James Hooton explains. 'If a Dingle is in despair, there's always a bed at the Dingle house.'

The glorified barn sits within a few acres of land, but lacks finesse, and even modcons like central heating. Downstairs there's an open-plan living and kitchen space, with a bar at one end, a section of The Woolpack's bar that the Dingles pilfered during a pub refit. Upstairs, there are four bedrooms and a self-contained flat, accessed by outside steps. The flat, first fashioned for Marlon and his dad Albert in 1996, was later the domain of Mandy Dingle, before it was renovated for Sam, Alice and Samson.

The Dingles' residence was first seen in 1994, when it was home to Zak, wife Nellie, and their grown-up children, Butch, Sam and Tina. The family faced their first fight the following year when, after they'd lived lived rent-free in the Holdgate Farm outbuildings for decades, owner Frank Tate tried to oust them. The Dingles drafted in the community to man the barricades as the Tates tried to enforce the eviction, with everyone eventually arrested. Fearing for the damage to his reputation, and horrified at the homeless Dingles camping out on his front lawn at Home Farm, Frank relented and issued them with a rent book. Now a proper dwelling, Nellie chose the name Wishing Well Cottage, after Zak and the boys took the old wishing well from The Woolpack, ripped out during the refit, and planted it in the front garden.

AFTER WIFE NELLIE walked out on the family to move to Ireland, Zak installed new girlfriend – and later wife – Lisa Clegg in the homestead. Christmas 1998 brought a surprise gift when Lisa went into labour in the pigsty, with vet Paddy helping to deliver the baby girl. Meanwhile, the Dingles' future again came under threat with Home Farm Estates' asset-stripping meaning Zak had to find £6,000 to buy the house. Much to Home Farm boss Lady Tara's surprise, the Dingles came up trumps, with Paddy's snobby mother Barbara giving the cash to Mandy, on the proviso she did not marry Paddy. Zak was keen to play down how 'middle class' he'd become now he was a homeowner, and when his brother Ezra arrived for Belle's christening in 1999, he was disgusted at Zak's status as 'house husband'.

2004 saw an epic gathering of Dingles for a huge party at Wishing Well, but Zak's pride soon led to a fall when he was riled by cousin, Solomon. Keen to win the title of 'King Dingle', Zak battled it out with Solomon in a contest, ultimately losing when Solomon cheated his way to victory. Desperate to get the homestead back, Zak and Lisa laid claim to their home, and eventually, after many rows and threats of fights, Solomon left.

The revolving door of Dingles at Wishing Well Cottage continued across the 2000s and 2010s, with Chas, Aaron, Debbie, Sarah, Cain, Delilah and Shadrach all living there at some point, the latter causing chaos in 2010 when he flooded the place. The Dingles' biggest challenge came in 2018, when Joe Tate tried to have Wishing Well demolished for a road to his new golf course. Once again, the Dingles manned barricades, but Joe tried a craftier approach and had bulldozers descend on the house, unaware that teenagers Samson and Noah were inside. Graham Foster and Eric Pollard managed to stop proceedings and rescue the boys, but the house was uninhabitable. Friends and family united to help the Dingles rebuild their damaged home, so they were soon back in their rightful place.

nowhere with Sam, Marlon made it to the wedding barn and was so shocked that he fainted. Marlon and Jessie married in a Caribbean-themed day, which culminated in the surprise return of Jessie's son, Billy, fresh from prison.

DAVID'S REVENGE
2015

David was out for teenager Lachlan White's blood after his sexual assault on David's wife, Alicia. David drove Lachlan to a barn, where he taunted and intimidated him. Broken, Lachlan confessed his crime, just as David's dad, Eric, and Alicia, found them and defused the situation.

THE MYSTERY LADY
2017

Young Sarah Sugden was surprised to find a woman staying in the Dingles' barn, and seeing that she was unwell, brought her food and money. The two bonded and when the woman collapsed, Sarah and the Dingles were shocked to discover it was Cain and Chas's long-lost mother, Faith, who was now homeless after donating all her money to Sarah's treatment fund.

MOIRA'S BARN BURNS
2017

Emma Barton finally confronted love rival Moira and confessed to having killed James. As they fought in Moira's barn, a pitchfork smashed a light, igniting a fire in the hay. Emma escaped, but as Moira went into labour, she begged for help. Emma crashed Moira's 4x4 into the barn, to provide an escape route, and the pair fled just as the barn exploded.

MARLON'S SURPRISE WEDDING
2018

Jessie Grant planned the perfect surprise for boyfriend Marlon: a secret Christmas Day wedding. After ending up in the middle of

PAUL'S ENDGAME
2021

Paul Ashdale was confronted by his son Vinny's girlfriend, Liv, on his wedding day to Mandy, as Liv pushed him to confess to his months of violent abuse towards Vinny. As Paul took his anger out on Liv, beating her, they were interrupted as Jimmy King crashed his van into the wedding barn, leaving Paul trapped when the building blew up and fatally injuring him.

Holdgate Farm

Originally a working farm, the roomy five-bedroom house was left empty in 1995 when its namesake, Mr Holdgate, died. Owner Frank Tate sought out new tenants, and the hardworking Glover family took the tenancy of Holdgate, finally securing a farm of their own, and working on a market garden in the polytunnels behind the house.

By 1999, the Glovers had disbanded, and the house was sold off to haulier, Sean Reynolds, and his wife Angie, who moved in with their teenage children, Marc and Ollie. After Sean and Angie's marriage collapsed, and Angie had died in 2002, the Marsden family moved in. After a brief stint in the house, the Marsdens left, with Tom King moving his sons in. In 2005, the Kings moved to Home Farm, leaving Alan and Terence Turner to take up residence.

Rodney Blackstock took ownership after Alan left, with ambitious plans to turn the property into a luxury spa for money-grabbing girlfriend Kelly Windsor and his son Paul Lambert. When Rodney's plans grew too expensive, Rodney offloaded the house onto Donald De Souza. Again, the De Souzas' tenure was a brief one; Donald died of a heart attack on the living-room floor in 2008. In early 2009, Holdgate Farm became the property of the Sharma family, who remain there to this day.

Holdgate Farm is one of several buildings where the interior is used for filming, rather than a studio set. While the real-life ground floor at Holdgate forms the Sharma's home on-screen, the upstairs of the house is multifunctional. The bedrooms of Holdgate Farm are redecorated and redressed as and when required, so they can be used as other sets, which over the years have included Priya's bedroom, Amba's nursery, Joe Tate's dressing room, Graham Foster's bedroom, various hotel rooms, and the room Rebecca White was held captive in by a nurse hired by Lachlan.

St Mary's Church

Emmerdale has supposedly had a church on the outskirts of the village since Beckindale Parish Church was formed in AD 989, but it wasn't until 2002 that it had a permanent set, as local churches had previously been borrowed for filming. When the Harewood set was constructed in 1997, a church and vicarage had been planned, but were scrapped due to the build budget. *Emmerdale* continued to use a real-life church until Zoe Tate burned down St. Mary's in 2002.

With the church destroyed, the old schoolhouse building, which was constructed on the village set, was repurposed. Kathy Glover had set up a tearoom there, later going into business with Eric Pollard as a wine bar, and then, with Marlon, as a diner. By 2002, the building was vacant and so became the parish church. 'I absolutely felt territorial, this was my set,' laughs John Middleton, who played Rev. Ashley Thomas. 'The church became a much more intimate space. It looks bigger than it really is on-screen. In reality, it's tiny, it's a chapel.'

Threatened with closure, despite protests, in 2008, the church was sold to Home Farm newcomers Mark and Natasha Wylde but, to the parishioners' relief, was returned to the community by Natasha – a move unpopular with her husband, given the £500,000 price tag! St. Mary's also survived a fire in 2009, caused by unhinged Sally Spode in her vendetta against Laurel Thomas, who was trapped inside, and managed to summon help by ringing the church bell. 'So many meaningful things that happened in the village happened in there – births, deaths, marriages,' John recalls. 'The big advantage of the show is the village set, no one else has got a backlot like that, and it makes it special for the characters in the show. The great dramas of their lives happen in that church set.'

FEATURE
VICARS OF THE PARISH

The village church has always needed a dependable and reliable vicar at the helm, and *Emmerdale* has seen no fewer than 13 members of the clergy during its 50 years.

REVEREND EDWARD RUSKIN
(George Little) 1972–75
The vicar since the 1960s, Reverend Ruskin left for a new parish in 1975.

REVEREND BOB MATTHEWS
(William Ellis) 1975–77
Reverend Matthews was met with initial hostility, given his youth, until Annie Sugden rallied the opposition to change their minds.

REVEREND WILLIAM HOCKLEY
(Jonathan Newth) 1977
One of several temporary vicars in the 1970s.

REVEREND DAVID COWPER
(John Abbott) 1977
Reverend Cowper brought trouble when his jilted bride plagued the village with nuisance phone calls.

REVEREND DONALD HINTON
(Hugh Manning) 1977–89
Particularly close to the Sugdens, Reverend Hinton was held hostage by Harry Mowlam's killer, Derek Warner, and persuaded him to confess. Hinton retired in 1989.

REVEREND TONY CHARLTON
(Stephen Rashbrook) 1990–91
Reverend Charlton had a keen interest in working with the younger people in the village.

REVEREND HAROLD BURNS
(David Hobbs) 1995–96
Reverend Burns was entrusted with conducting Joe Sugden's funeral.

REVEREND ASHLEY THOMAS
(John Middleton) 1996–2012, 2014–16
Emmerdale's longest-serving and best-loved vicar, who left following his dementia diagnosis.

ETHAN BLAKE
(Liam O'Brien) 2003–5, 2006
Ethan was a curate who worked with Ashley. Ethan kissed Debbie Dingle, earning him a beating from her father, Cain. He then had a thing for Kelly Windsor, before trying to break up Ashley and Laurel.

REVEREND JUDE WATSON
(Andy Wear) 2012–14
Jude took over after Ashley resigned, following his abuse of his elderly father, Sandy.

REVEREND HARRIET FINCH
(Katherine Dow Blyton) 2014, 2016–2021
Former police officer Harriet was a popular addition to the church, but suffered knocks to her faith.

RHYS
(Sam Alexander) 2018
A temporary vicar, nephew of Bishop Barry, who took over when Harriet left in 2018. Unpopular with the villagers, they mounted a KHAV group (Keep Harriet as Vicar).

CHARLES ANDERSON
(Kevin Mathurin) 2020–Present
Non-stipendiary Minister Charles saved the day by stepping in to marry Chas and Paddy on Christmas Day 2020. Charles has remained a support and confidant to the villagers since.

Reverend Ashley Thomas

1996–2017 / Played by John Middleton

'I'm meant to listen while people unburden their guilt onto me. They get to ease their conscience and to seek forgiveness. I have to keep soaking it up.'
Ashley Thomas

While *Emmerdale* had always had a vicar, the role was largely confined to baptizing the newborn, marrying the betrothed and burying the dead – but then Reverend Ashley Thomas arrived. 'I was only brought in for about six episodes. I was told to be prepared to be around when needed for hatch, match and dispatch,' John Middleton explains. 'Then a scene went out between me and Samantha Giles, where she is flirting with me, and the idea was to have him lovelorn and pining for Bernice, and that's when the character started to kick off.'

Ashley's vocation was an obvious main aspect to his character, but his success in becoming a fully rounded, long-standing character lay beyond his faith. 'What the writers needed to do was see beyond the dog collar and see him as a man,' John says. 'And the interesting thing was then, when you were writing his relationships, you're not writing for two people, you're writing for three because God's in there somewhere.'

Having to face many traumas across the years meant Ashley's faith was knocked, but this made for interesting playing for John. 'I did find that fascinating, playing someone with a deep and devout religion, because it always gives this tension between what he ought not to be doing and what he should be doing.' One of Ashley's toughest tests of character

was when he became abusive to his elderly father, Sandy, even hitting him in frustration. 'I was never happy with the story where Ashley turned on his father, I felt that was completely out of character,' John considers. 'But I said to Charlotte (Laurel) "we're taxi drivers, we may not like where we're going but we'll get them there".'

Not a natural lothario, Ashley had a tough time when it came to romance, but having been ditched by Bernice, and left holding baby Gabby, he finally found his true equal, the love of his life: Laurel. 'It was the reverse of how Ashley felt about Bernice – Laurel felt this about Ashley and he was unaware of it at the beginning, so he had to move heaven and earth to get to her, which he did,' John explains. Despite the couple breaking up – with Laurel even going on to marry Marlon – Laurel and Ashley reunited when he was faced with his biggest ever challenge: dementia. 'I thought that had a beautiful resolution. As the dementia story played out what we were telling was a tragic love story, because they had re-engaged, and he realized he couldn't do it without her. That made it a moving story.'

Edna Birch

2000–15 / Played by Shirley Stelfox

'To a life lived with courage and strength, to Edna Birch, a finer woman we'll never know.'
Jimmy King

In her trademark hat and coat, Edna Birch was a fierce, God-fearing little lady, unafraid to take anyone on and put them in their place, from man of the cloth Ashley to shady businessman Tom King. 'I shared a dressing room with Shirley, she'd always have to have Edna's shoes, Edna's hat. She was a great character,' Charlotte Bellamy recalls.

A devout, churchgoing Christian, Edna was a pillar of the community, and an instantly recognizable character. 'Everything about her was accurate – the way she dressed, the way she behaved, what she said,' Tony Audenshaw adds. 'She twice took her hat off – once doing ballroom dancing and once when she had a fall, and it was so profound.'

However, this good Samaritan had more than her fair share of skeletons in the closet. Her troublesome granddaughter Eve came to stay with Edna on a few occasions, but as it turned out, Eve was not Edna's grandchild, but her great-niece. Edna's 'son' Peter was in reality her nephew – Edna's sister Lily had had a child out of wedlock and Edna and her husband, Harold, raised the boy as their own. But this wasn't Edna's only family

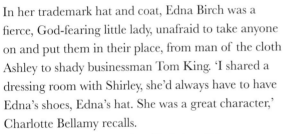

secret – her husband had had an affair with a man, Lawrence White, in the 1960s. As homosexuality was illegal at the time, she reported them to the police and Lawrence was imprisoned. Edna had gone decades believing he'd died, before coming face to face with him, when he moved his family to Home Farm in 2014.

Shirley Stelfox passed away in 2015, as did her character the following year, and the village mourned her loss. 'It's horrible, to do the fictional death when the actor has died. Edna's death was awful to do, Shirley was such a loss to the show,' writer Bill Lyons recalls. 'Edna was a fabulous character to write, because she could say what everybody else was thinking, she could be tactless and say all the things you wanted to put in an episode.' For many, Shirley's portrayal of Edna created their favourite character, 'It was a great privilege to work with her, she taught me many, many things,' Nick Miles reminisces. 'She never held anything up, never took a sick day, she'd never take a mark through fear she'd glance down and look at it, and I try to emulate that.'

The Cemetery

The only soap to boast a permanent village cemetery, the Emmerdale graveyard is where many characters have been laid to rest over the years. While some 'graves' are those of characters – ranging from Jacob Sugden, whose funeral took place in the first episode, through to Leanna Cavanagh, who died in 2021 – some are grouped in family plots, like the Tates, Dingles and Kings. Not all of the graves belong to *Emmerdale* characters, however – when the village set was constructed in 1997, real headstones were salvaged from an East London graveyard when it was redeveloped. In addition, two small headstones – to Timothy J Fee and Mike Long – are the fictional graves of previous crew members; Tim as the long-standing former production controller, and Mike the designer responsible for the creation of the Harewood village set.

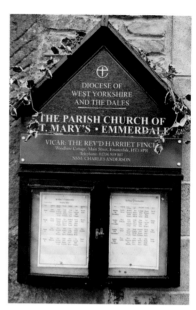

KEY

1. Mike Long
2. Tim Fee
3. Joanie Dingle
4. Elizabeth Pollard
5. Alan Turner
6. Tricia Dingle
7. Mary King / Max King
8. Tom King
9. Matthew King
10. Carl King
11. Vic Windsor
12. Donna Windsor
13. Bill Whiteley
14. Sarah Sugden
15. Sam Pearson
16. Pat Sugden
17. Meg Armstrong
18. Jacob Sugden
19. Henry Wilks
20. Joe Sugden
21. Liam Hammond
22. Frank Tate / Chris Tate
23. Dave Glover / Linda Glover
24. Rachel Hughes
25. Angie Reynolds
26. Edith Weatherall
27. Terry Woods
28. Seth Armstrong
29. Dawn Woods
30. Ben Dingle / Butch Dingle
31. Leanna Cavanagh
32. James Barton
33. Finn Barton
34. Ashley Thomas
35. Daniel Doland Thomas
36. Edna Birch
37. Paul Ashdale
38. Emma Barton
39. Val Pollard
40. Gennie Walker
41. Grace Dingle
42. Katie Sugden
43. Robbie Lawson
44. Alice Dingle
45. Len Reynolds
46. Jack Sugden
47. Mark Wylde
48. Jackson Walsh

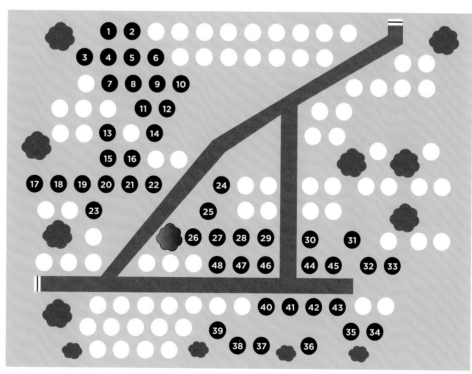

Smithy Cottage

An imposing detached house at the top of the village, Smithy Cottage was originally, as its namesake suggests, the village blacksmith. The three-bedroom house is usually lived in by whoever holds the vets' practice in the annexe, and in 1995 it proved the perfect first home for vet Zoe Tate and her girlfriend, Emma Nightingale. After Zoe and Emma's relationship ended, Zoe was joined by fellow vet Paddy Kirk, before allowing Paddy and new wife Mandy to rent Smithy Cottage.

Paddy and Mandy's marriage did not last; she had an affair with her father's carer, and Paddy got into a relationship with Emily Dingle. Paddy and Emily married and began fostering, and Debbie Jones, who would later be revealed as Charity and Cain's long-lost love child, was just one of the children they took in. When Zoe left for New Zealand in 2005, she sold the house to Paddy.

For a time, Paddy's on-off girlfriend Chas Dingle lived at Smithy, bringing along her troublesome son, Aaron. When vet Rhona Goskirk returned to the village in 2010, both Paddy and Marlon were smitten, but Rhona eventually settled down with Paddy – after a relationship with Marlon. Rhona discovered she was pregnant with Marlon's child, and after coming to terms with the news that her baby would be born with Down's syndrome, Rhona reached an agreement with Paddy and Marlon that the three of them would bring up Leo, born in 2011.

Paddy and Rhona married, but after he cheated on her with Leo's teaching assistant, they divorced – Paddy getting the vets' surgery shares and Rhona getting the house in the settlement. Rhona continues to live at Smithy Cottage with Leo, now with Marlon, and his daughter, April.

'God bless The Woolpack, and all that drink in her!'
Diane Sugden

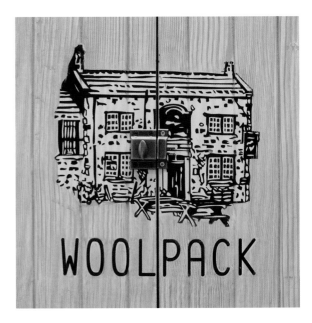

POST-WAR, AMOS BREARLY took on the tenancy of The Woolpack, running it alone. Thinking the brewery wanted a couple at the helm, he proposed to recently widowed Annie Sugden, who turned him down. Instead, Amos teamed up with wealthy former mill owner Henry Wilks, who'd invested in Emmerdale Farm, and the pair bought the freehold from Ephraim Monk. Amos and Henry ran the pub for the next 18 years – Henry joining Amos in the living quarters from 1973, after his house burned down.

In 1976 the pair rehoused The Woolpack, after a large crack in the fireplace exposed subsidence. Amos and Henry found new premises, in a derelict corn chandler's building. After Amos suffered a stroke in 1991, he and Henry decided to sell, and former Home Farm boss Alan Turner bought the place. Turner played at the convivial host for the next eight years, relishing his social standing in the community. Turner helped develop The Woolpack's food offering, later taking on Marlon Dingle as chef – a move that would ensure Marlon's presence in the pub for nearly 25 years. Turner embarked on a revamp in 1995, bringing in Zoe Tate's girlfriend, Emma Nightingale, an interior designer, to oversee the modernization of the bar area. Having sought investment from the brewery, Alan had to take the business in a more corporate direction, starting with hiring married couple Terry and Britt Woods as managers, before their marriage later collapsed. By 1998, Alan had been joined by long-lost granddaughter Tricia Stokes, who was partly responsible for the fire that gutted the pub while she was looking after the place with Terry.

While The Woolpack was refurbished, the brewery sent in agency barmaid Bernice Blackstock to run a temporary bar in the village hall. Bernice would later return as bar manager when the pub reopened.

Following a heart attack, Turner decided to sell up in 1999, and Bernice and her fiancé, Gavin Ferris, bought it for £250,000, after Bernice's wealthy friend Stella Jones gave her the £75,000 deposit. Gavin had a fling with Paddy's cousin, Jason, on the eve of the wedding, leaving Bernice devastated. Bernice called off the engagement and her mother, Diane, sold her Brighton B&B and bought out Gavin's share.

Bernice left in 2002, selling her share to Louise Appleton. The 2003 storm damaged the pub when lightning hit the roof and the chimney collapsed – damaging the bar and sending part of the front wall showering down onto Tricia Dingle below, fatally injuring her. The Woolpack was repaired, and in 2006 Louise sold her share to Diane's sister, Val. Val and Diane's partnership was rocky, and Diane bought her out in 2009. By 2010, Diane wanted to sell, having lost her savings and a loan against the pub to conman Charlie Haynes. Nicola and Jimmy King were initially interested, but they pulled out when they realized it was too much hard work. When barmaid Chas Dingle offered to buy half, Diane agreed. Their partnership was cut short in 2015 when Chas, suffering from PTSD, stabbed Diane in the back room of the pub while sleepwalking. Diane recovered, the act ironically saving her life as surgery uncovered the return of cancer. Diane fought into remission but decided to retire from pub life, selling her share to Chas's second cousin, Charity, who was recently released from prison.

Charity ran the pub with Chas until 2021 when her self-destructive antics reached a head and Chas persuaded her to sell her share to her cousin, Marlon, who had for over 20 years been in charge of the kitchen at The Woolpack. Financial difficulties in the wake of COVID and a slow return to normality meant Chas and Marlon were forced to take on investment from enemy, Al Chapman, who made secretive moves to bankrupt the business and redevelop it as luxury flats. Meeting opposition from Marlon and Chas, Al blew The Woolpack up in a gas explosion on Christmas Day 2021. The following year, Charity took over again, with financial help from son Ryan and The Woolpack rose from the ashes.

FEATURE
WOOLPACK STAFF

'As an actor, filming in the pub is when we get to see each other, it's our catch-up day. It's the heart of the village. When you're there, you feel at the core or heart of the story.' **Lisa Riley** *(Mandy Dingle)*

LANDLORDS & LANDLADIES: Amos Brearly (1948–73), Amos Brearly/Henry Wilks (1973–91), Alan Turner (1991–99), Bernice Blackstock/Gavin Ferris (1999), Bernice Blackstock/Diane Sugden (1999–2002), Diane Sugden/Louise Appleton (2002–06), Diane Sugden/Val Pollard (2006–09), Diane Sugden (2009–10) Nicola King/Jimmy King (2010), Diane Sugden/Chas Dingle (2010–15), Chas Dingle/Charity Dingle (2016–21), Chas Dingle/Marlon Dingle/Al Chapman (2021), Charity Dingle/Ryan Stocks (2022)

MANAGERS: Terry Woods, Britt Woods, Chas Dingle

BAR STAFF: Alison Gibbons, Mick Caven, Dolly Acaster, Carol Nelson, Archie Brooks, Caroline Bates, Lynn Whiteley, Elizabeth Feldmann, Sarah Sugden, Kathy Glover, Shirley Turner, Rachel Hughes, Biff Fowler, Jan Glover, Susie Wilde, Mandy Dingle, Tricia Stokes, Jason Kirk, Tonicha Daggert, Paul Lambert, Katie Addyman, Bob Hope, Jasmine Thomas, Lexi Nicholls, Jo Sugden, Moira Barton, Maisie Wylde, Priya Sharma, Mick Naylor, Debbie Dingle, Cameron Murray, Ashley Thomas, Alicia Metcalfe, Doug Potts, Finn Barton, James Barton, Jermaine Bailey, Rebecca White, Matty Barton, Faith Dingle, Dawn Taylor, Bear Wolf, Ellis Chapman

KITCHEN STAFF: Mark Hughes, Marlon Dingle, Carlos Diaz, Jake Doland, Victoria Sugden, Thomas King, Luke Posner

CLEANERS: Winnie Purvis, Betty Eagleton, Heather Hutchinson, Rachel Breckle, Lydia Hart, Nellie Dingle

Amos Brearly & Henry Wilks

1972–95 & 1972–91 / Played by Ronald Magill
& Arthur Pentelow

'Us old 'uns have got a few innings left in us yet, 'ey?'
'I certainly hope so, Henry.'
Henry Wilks & Amos Brearly

With his distinctive bushy sideburns, Amos Brearly was the gruff, seemingly dour landlord of The Woolpack, running the hostelry as he saw fit since 1948. On the opposite side of the coin was Henry Wilks, the prosperous, retired, Bradford mill owner, viewed with suspicion by the village when he first retired to Beckindale in 1972. The reality was that both men were kindhearted – particularly towards people like Annie, Dolly and Sarah – generous, and always ready with a friendly ear to listen to troubles – or gossip. Henry invested in The Woolpack in 1973, enabling him and Amos to buy the freehold from the brewery, and so began an unlikely duo of iconic characters; the original *Emmerdale* double act.

The pipe-smoking pair kept an orderly pub with clear rules and were reluctant to change; in the age of the microchip even a Space Invaders machine and a microwave seemed too radical. With strong opinions, the pair would bicker and argue, but despite the petty conflict at times, they grew to become friends and companions – even though Amos would be a stickler for referring to Henry as 'Mr Wilks' throughout.

Amos, a collector of junk, was also a roving reporter for the *Hotten Courier*, often seen at his typewriter in the back room of the pub, shirking his responsibilities at the bar. Henry had a daughter, Marian, who lived in Italy, but Amos remained devoid of any family, although his persistence with Annie Sugden paid off when they finally married in 1995.

Amos retired in 1991, following a stroke, and the 18-year partnership with Mr Wilks came to an end as they sold up to Alan Turner. Henry passed away soon after, following the real-life death of Arthur Pentelow, with Amos returning to pay tribute to his friend. While Amos' status is officially unknown since moving to Spain with Annie, Ronald Magill passed away in 2007. 'They were absolute superstars, they were done by all the impressionists! They really were so welcoming, they made everything into a laugh,' Malandra Burrows remembers. 'They'd share all their stories, they were wonderful people.'

WOODBINE COTTAGE

Second in the row of cottages on the left side of Main Street is Woodbine Cottage, originally the home of Edna Birch and her dog, Batley. Batley died in 2002, and is buried in the front garden, with Edna later finding a new companion in dog Tootsie. Edna enjoyed the company of lodgers across the years, including Pearl Ladderbanks, Ashley Thomas and his father Sandy, Paddy Kirk, Edna's sister, Lily, and Edna's granddaughter, Eve. From 2015, police-officer-turned-vicar Harriet Finch has been a permanent resident. In recent years Harriet has reconnected with Will Taylor, with whom she was in a relationship years previously and after they settled their differences Will moved in, adding his recovering addict daughter Dawn and her young son, Lucas.

BUTLERS FARM

Having left Emmerdale Farm in 2002, the Sugdens took on the 157-acre Butlers Farm. Initially Andy and Katie's domain, Andy later ran it with second wife, Jo. After their marriage collapsed, Andy lost the tenancy of the farm to the Bartons. Since 2009, Moira Barton, now Dingle, has ensured the survival of the farm. Following husband John's death, Moira took his brother, James, into the business, until his death. Moira has relied on the graft of several farm hands, including Sam Dingle, Eve Jenson, Pete Barton, Alex Moss and Nate Robinson – the last three all having had flings with Moira. The four-bedroom farmhouse is the family home of Moira and Cain, her son Matty, his son Kyle, and their son Isaac. The farm, worth one million pounds, is owned primarily by Moira, but Rhona also owns a share, as do Pete and Ross Barton. With a strong beef herd, Butlers supplies many businesses, including The Woolpack, David's Shop, The Hide and several restaurants in Hotten.

MULBERRY COTTAGE

Originally the village police station, and first seen on-screen as a B&B, Mulberry Cottage was home to Simon Meredith and Nicola Blackstock in 2004. By 2007, the house was used as the new vicarage, with Ashley moving in with his family – Laurel, Gabby, Jasmine, Arthur and Doug. The house came under threat in 2008 when it went on the market, but new Home Farm owners Mark and Natasha Wylde purchased it and continued to rent to the Thomases. When their marriage fell apart, Ashley and Laurel left, and the house was sold to Debbie Dingle. Following Debbie's departure in 2015, Ashley and Laurel returned to the house, the familiarity helping Ashley, who was in the throes of dementia. Baby Dotty was born in the house in 2016, and Ashley passed away in the living room the following year. Laurel remains at four-bedroomed Mulberry, living with children Arthur and Dotty, her partner Jai and his son Archie.

BROOK COTTAGE

The first house at the top right of Main Street is detached, three-bedroom Brook Cottage. First seen as the home of lawyer Laura Johnstone, and later Zoe Tate, the cottage was then used as the vicarage – for Ashley, niece Jasmine, father Sandy and wife Laurel. Brook was gutted in a fire in 2007, and after repair it became home to Carrie and Scarlett Nicholls. Rodney Blackstock was next to set up home, renting from Home Farm Estates, before the notorious Spencer family landed in the village. Over the next few years, Brook housed several tenants, from Megan Macey and son Robbie, Dominic Andrews and his daughter Gemma, and Harriet Finch and Ashley, following his break-up with Laurel. Most recently, the cottage has been home to Diane, Bernice and their family, with Diane also having taken pity on Charity, following her exile from The Woolpack.

TUG GHYLL

Next door to Woodbine Cottage is Tug Ghyll. First home to Jarvis Skelton, Scott Windsor bought the house in 2005. When Scott moved abroad, Debbie Dingle bought it, living there with on-off girlfriend Jasmine. By 2009, Debbie had a house full: with daughter Sarah, dad Cain, mum Charity and young brother Noah all living in the tiny three-bedroom cottage. After Charity and Cain both left, and Debbie had had baby Jack, Debbie looked for a fresh start from the memories of murderous ex, Cameron, and moved to bigger Mulberry Cottage. The house was sold to Katie Sugden, using the settlement from her divorce from Declan. After Katie died in 2015, husband Andy inherited the house and rented it to a string of tenants, including Leyla Harding, Vanessa Woodfield, Carly Hope, Frank Clayton, Tracy Metcalfe and Maya Stepney. By 2020, Tracy had

settled with boyfriend Nate Robinson, and the couple were joined by baby Frankie the following year.

DALE HEAD

The last house on the left of Main Street, Dale Head featured for several years on the show without the inside ever being seen, before Declan Macey bought and renovated it in 2010 to live in. After he moved to Home Farm, he rented Dale Head to Hazel Rhodes and her son, Jackson, Declan paying to have the house adapted for disabled Jackson's needs. After Jackson's assisted suicide, Hazel left Emmerdale, and Dale Head has been home ever since to Dan Spencer and his daughter Amelia. Originally joined by girlfriend Kerry Wyatt, Dan threw her out in 2020 after she cheated on him. Dan occasionally takes in lodgers – recently brother Daz, and also Will Taylor and Harriet Finch, to help him pay the rent to Home Farm Estates.

KEEPERS COTTAGE

This cosy three-bedroom cottage next to the café was originally home to legendary couple Seth and Betty, who lived there from 1995 to 2003. The pair took in various lodgers over the years, including Paddy Kirk, Terry Woods and Biff Fowler, the latter buying the house from Home Farm Estates to prevent Seth and Betty being evicted in 1998. Betty stayed on after Seth's death and continued to take in lodgers to satisfy her nose for gossip, including Alan Turner, Laurel Potts, Sandy Thomas and Victoria Sugden. Victoria used her inheritance from Jack to buy the house at a modestly priced £60,000 and after Betty's departure, moved in boyfriend – later husband – Adam Barton. After Adam went on the run, Victoria was joined at Keepers by friends Rebecca White, then later Amy and Kerry Wyatt, and then her young son Harry.

VICTORIA COTTAGE

Next to Keepers is Victoria Cottage, originally tied with Home Farm, and the residence of Caroline Bates – first with her children Nick and Kathy, then later with Alan Turner. Eric Pollard moved into the house in 1992 with wife Elizabeth, then lived there with wife Dee, before swapping homes with Kathy Glover, who moved in with niece Alice. Kathy left for Australia in 2001 and Victoria became home to several couples; first Marlon and Tricia, then Paul and Siobhan Marsden, and finally Matthew and Sadie King. Home Farm Estates then took ownership, renting to several friends over the years, including Leyla, Gennie, Katie, Vanessa and Chas. Rakesh Kotecha bought the house in 2014, moving in with wife Priya, her daughter Amba, and Rakesh's son, Kirin. In a money-making scheme, Rakesh swapped for Mill Cottage, and the Kings moved to Victoria, crammed into the small house from 2015 through to today.

DALE VIEW

Originally the holiday home of Ms Curtis, Dale View became the on-off marital home of Roy and Kelly Glover in 1999, before becoming the property of Home Farm Estates. Notorious for being a house for sharers, Dale View has housed Nicola, Chloe, Syd and Chas, various King family members, Sam and son Samson, and finally mates Daz Eden and Jake Doland. Andy Sugden became the long-time tenant from 2010 after giving up Butlers Farm, joined over the years by various mates and girlfriends, before Dale View became home to the Barton family. First Ross, Pete and Finn, then the lads were joined by their parents. The Bartons had left by 2018, leaving Home Farm Estates to rent to Wendy Posner and her son Luke, who later took in Andrea and Millie Tate as co-tenants for a time.

TENANT HOUSE

One of the most lived-in cottages in the village, Tenant House, originally informally known as Annie's Cottage, is one of the oldest buildings, with the date on the lintel showing 1671. After selling Emmerdale Farm, Annie moved to Tenant House in 1993, retiring to Spain the following year. The house was rented out; first to the Glovers, then the Sugdens, then the Cairns family. Jack allowed several singletons to move in across the years, including Biff Fowler, Marlon Dingle, Terry Woods, Will Cairns, Jed Outhwaite, Sean Rossi, Carlos Diaz, Sean Reynolds, Pete Collins and Richie Carter. Finally, in 2002, the cottage became home to the Sugdens again, after they lost their farm. After discovering the truth about her mother's death, Victoria set fire to the house in 2007, and when the insurance company refused to pay out, Jack sold to the Dolands. Greg, Mel and Jake's tenure was short as Greg and Mel left after the baby swap meant their baby had died, not Ashley and Laurel's.

Faye and Ryan Lamb moved in next, Faye looking to put pressure on husband Mark, who had abandoned them decades previously and assumed a new identity. After Faye left, Jai bought Tenant House for Rachel Breckle, who was pregnant with his child. Rachel's family later joined in her. By 2015, Rachel and the Spencers had moved on and Megan Macey moved in, initially with Sam and Samson Dingle, and later her partner Frank. Following Frank's death, Megan left for Newcastle, and in 2020 Jai rented the house to Dr Liam Cavanagh, who lived there first with Leanna, and then wife Leyla.

CONNELTON VIEW

Briefly owned by unhinged killer Graham Clark, Connelton View became home to Chloe Atkinson, and later Brian and Katie Addyman, before Dawn, Terry and baby TJ Woods set up there from 2003. Terry and TJ remained in the house after Dawn's death, then were later joined by Brenda Walker, Terry's partner. After Terry's death in 2011, TJ went to live with his grandmother in Morocco and Brenda stayed on at Connelton View, with Rodney Blackstock as lodger. Eventually Brenda found love with Bob Hope and he moved in, with his twins Cathy and Heath. Bob and the kids still live in the house, while Brenda has recently taken up with Eric Pollard.

JACOBS FOLD

Initially home to the Daggerts, who squatted in the empty house, Jacobs Fold then became home to Len Reynolds.and partner Pearl Ladderbanks, until Len's death in 2007 when Pearl discovered Len had sold the house to Eric Pollard. Pearl remained at Jacobs Fold until 2015, when Eric paid her off to move out, so he could start charging higher rent. First home to Kirin, and then Chrissie and Lachlan White, Eric sparked a bidding war when he put the house up for auction, and it was bought by Joe Tate, posing as Tom Waterhouse, for an overpriced £350,000. Joe had bought the house for girlfriend Debbie Dingle and her family, with Charity and Vanessa and their sons having joined for a time while Debbie was away in Scotland. Charity continues to live here with Sarah and Noah, renting from Home Farm Estates.

TALL TREES COTTAGE

Originally a pair of houses on the edge of the cricket field, Tall Trees Cottage was left to Val Pollard after owner Noreen Bell died in 2006. Val sold to Marlon Dingle, who lived there first with wife Donna, then third wife Laurel and her family, and then fourth wife Jessie and her grown-up sons. Marlon was rocked by the news that he had a daughter, April, who came to live with him permanently from 2014, after the death of Donna. Marlon and April have been joined over the years by several family members and friends, but moved out in 2021 to set up home with Marlon's partner, Rhona. Since then Tall Trees has been a lads' pad for sharers Billy Fletcher, Ellis Chapman, Ryan Stocks and Mackenzie Boyd.

FARRERS BARN

A large stone barn split in two – one side for a business, originally Pollard's Antiques and now David's Shop, and the other a three-bedroom cottage. The house was for years home to Eric Pollard, joined initially by wife Gloria, then son David, and eventually fourth wife Val. Eric hit financial difficulties in 2010 and sold the barn to David. David has remained there since, running the shop next door, and has set up home with various wives and girlfriends, including Leyla Harding, Alicia Gallagher, Priya Sharma, Tracy Shankley, Maya Stepney, Meena Jutla and Victoria Sugden. A constant throughout has been David's teenage stepson, Jacob Gallagher, and David's baby son Theo, dumped on his doorstep on Christmas Day 2019 by Maya.

Mill Cottage

Mill Cottage started off as a semi-derelict water mill, on the edge of Emmerdale Farm's land. Jack Sugden briefly took up residence in 1972, but it would be 1986 before Mill was next seen. Sandie Merrick and her builder boyfriend Phil Pearce bought the place to renovate it, with Sandie taking ownership when she and Phil split, first moving in Kate Hughes and her children, and then Dolly and Sam Skilbeck, before she sold to Frank Tate in 1991.

Frank gave the house as a wedding gift to son Chris. Chris lived at Mill first with Kathy, then second wife Rachel. By 2001, Ray Mullan had snapped up Mill, but his tenure was brief, since his girlfriend Louise Appleton soon accidentally killed him. Rodney Blackstock then got his hands on the luxury five-bedroomed house, moving his much younger girlfriend, Kelly Windsor, and his son, Paul Lambert, in.

In 2006, Rodney faced financial ruin and lost Mill Cottage, which was bought by solicitor Grayson Sinclair for a million pounds. Grayson moved in with wife Perdita. After the marriage collapsed, Carl King bought the house, with the rest of the family joining him when they lost their empire. Following Carl's death in 2012, Jimmy inherited the house, but in 2015, while Nicola was away in Dubai, cash-strapped Jimmy sold the house to Rakesh Kotecha for a miniscule £285,000. Rakesh looked to convert Mill into luxury apartments, but when he ran out of cash, he burned the property down for the insurance.

The burned-out remains of Mill Cottage were repossessed and went to auction, with Aaron Dingle using his and half-sister Liv's inheritance from their father to secure the house. Aaron and Liv renovated the building into two plush apartments, and while they lived in one, the second is currently occupied by Charles Anderson and Manpreet Sharma.

Home Farm

Desirable, affluent and palatial, Home Farm should be the des res of the Dales, but this sprawling manor is the poisoned chalice of Emmerdale, plagued to bring each of its families misery and misfortune.

    With a multi-million-pound price tag, the 'big house on the hill' has undergone many changes across the years, from admin hub of agricultural company NY Estates, through to Joe Tate's playboy mansion, but today it still retains its 'estate' status: holding game shoots, corporate events, weddings and parties, owning hundreds of acres of land, several tenant farms and myriad properties in the village. The eleven-bedroom manor house is currently Kim Tate's domain, 'It's kind of her spiritual home. She loved that house, the horses, the land,' Claire King explains. 'When she fled, I think she was probably always thinking of coming back some day. She liked the power, the status symbol. I think that's where her heart is.'

    The coveted property, a symbol of aspiration and ambition, is important for the show's dynamics, 'Home Farm is essential,' believes *Emmerdale* writer, Bill Lyons. 'There should be the big folk on the hill who can mess up your life. When Chris Tate propositioned Linda Glover, he said "I own you, your job is down to me, your husband's job is down to me, your house is down to me". It's that feeling that what happens in the big house affects everyone down below.'

    However, Home Farm's rich (in all senses of the word) occupants have across the years proved that money does not buy happiness. The curse of Home Farm has claimed many lives, caused many fights and squabbles – usually money fuelled – and has seen the destruction of many Emmerdale families, resulting in an unforgettable history to Emmerdale's most expensive address.

'It makes you wonder if it's the building: Home Farm. Such terrible things have happened there, indecent people, doing indecent things – you wonder if somehow the house is responsible for the bad things.'
Alan Turner

HOME FARM STARTED life as the Miffield Hall Estate, the ancestral home of the Verney family. Their outdated feudal system of ruling over the working classes of the village came to an end in 1978, when George Verney died. With mounting debts, his family sold, and the estate became known as Home Farm, now the property of NY Estates. The company sent a string of estate managers to implement new farming techniques to the Dales. The most notable of managers came in the shape of Alan Turner, who arrived to run Home Farm in 1982. Alan would prove a popular addition and a pillar of the community. His stint at running Home Farm, which had later changed to joint ownership with Joe Sugden, ended when it was sold to Frank Tate, in 1989, for £1 million.

The Tates' ownership lasted ten years, during which Frank, Kim and Chris built up the estate, with an emphasis on the tourism and leisure industries. After infighting took control out of their hands and to local toff Lady Tara Oakwell, she sold it on to lottery winner Stella Jones in 1999. Stella's stay was brief,

and after she tired of money-grabbing villagers, she sold Home Farm back to the Tates.

The Tates' time at Home Farm ended when Zoe emigrated in 2005, but not before she destroyed the house in a gas explosion as revenge on new owner Tom King, for blackmailing her into selling at a reduced price. It was only a matter of time before Home Farm's curse struck the Kings, firstly when Tom's youngest son was killed, and then when Tom himself was murdered. The King brothers inherited the estate, but when their business collapsed in 2008, it was repossessed and sold to Mark and Natasha Wylde. The Wylde's happiness was ill-fated and after Mark was outed as a bigamist, Natasha shot him dead. Their son, Nathan, was conned into selling the estate for £4.25 million, to Declan Macey. Declan's time as lord of the manor was no better: he first discovered he wasn't the father of his daughter, Mia, who then died in a car crash; then he faced losing his business empire. Suicidal Declan burned the house down, saved at the last minute by Charity, who suggested rebuilding the empire with the insurance money.

When the insurance fraud was uncovered, Home Farm was sold to Lawrence White. The Whites had a turbulent few years, before planning to leave for Australia, but the entire family was involved in a car crash, killing Lawrence and his daughter Chrissie. With Joe Tate as the new owner, the Tates' reign returned to Home Farm, although he was later revealed to be a proxy for Kim. After nearly 20 years' absence, Kim came home, later tracking down her long-lost son Jamie and allowing him and his young family to join her in their rightful place at Home Farm.

A large house like Home Farm has needed the help of staff across the years. Several gamekeepers have kept poachers at bay, or in some cases, kept the poaching to themselves – most famously Seth Armstrong , as well as Zak and Sam Dingle, with Sam's wife Lydia, currently 'doing' for the Tates inside the house. Home Farm has seen several housekeepers, including Tina Dingle, Pearl Ladderbanks and Dolly Skilbeck. Jean Rogers remembers fondly, 'I always felt that Kim and Dolly had a good relationship. Kim was very supportive of Dolly because of the way she took to the responsibility and dealt with functions. When Dolly did go off to Norfolk, I've always thought Dolly ran her own establishment where there's wedding functions.'

The longest-serving *Emmerdale* set, Home Farm is in reality Creskeld Hall, near the Emmerdale village set at Harewood. Exteriors are still filmed at the property, including specifically added façades for the 1996 fire that claimed Dave Glover's life, the 2005 gas explosion and Tom King's murder in 2006. For the 2013 Christmas Day fire, a specially commissioned façade was created in the grounds of *Emmerdale's* set at Harewood.

Home Farm has undergone several versions of studio set for its interiors, including several tweaks to its layout. 'We're very lucky because it's a large set and you can do so much with it,' explains Claire King, 'You can film right through the three rooms. It's definitely my favourite set. It still doesn't get cleaned any better than the other sets, though! There's a lot of dust around; that Lydia doesn't do a good job!'

CHAPTER 3

THE CHARACTERS

'You have the whole of society in a small village, and ever-changing drama every day, and viewers want to unwind and see a drama unfold in front of you and you buy into the characters that are representing life. It's entertainment.'

James Hooton *(Sam Dingle)*

Over 450 main characters have graced the village of Emmerdale since the show began. Some have passed through, many have remained for years, or decades. Whole family units, spanning several generations, have arrived or been born, and have died or exited. Some are victims, others are villains. Some you love, some you love to hate. Some you root for, others you want to see get their comeuppance. One thing's for sure in *Emmerdale*, there's something, and someone, to appeal to every viewer, ensuring that life in the village is never short of drama for its inhabitants.

The Sugdens

1972-Present

'There have always been farmers in the Sugden family – and long may it continue.'
Jack Sugden

The original Dales' family, and archetypal farming folk, the Sugdens' family tree was fairly straightforward back in 1972. Widowed Annie Sugden (Sheila Mercier) and her father, Sam Pearson (Toke Townley), lived and worked at Emmerdale Farm with son Joe (Frazer Hines), daughter Peggy (Jo Kendall) and Peggy's husband Matt (Freddie Pyne). Black sheep of the family, eldest son Jack (Andrew Burt/Clive Hornby) would make a brief return, but as an established novelist, farm life was not for him.

The family was joined by twins Sam and Sally in 1973, when Peggy gave birth, but by 1976 they had all tragically died. Bereaved Matt found happiness again when he married Dolly Acaster (Katharine Barker/ Jean Rogers) in 1978, having the child they always

yearned for in 1982, when son Samuel (Benjamin Whitehead) was born. Joe meanwhile found brief happiness with wife Christine Sharp (Angela Cheyne), but the marriage collapsed after only a few weeks.

Jack made a permanent return to the farm in 1980 and reconciled with ex-lover Pat (Lynn Dalby/ Helen Weir) who he'd marry in 1982, following the revelation that her teenage son Jackie (Ian Sharrock) was in fact Jack's biological son. Annie's father, Sam, passed away in 1984, as did Pat in 1986, shortly after the birth of son Robert (Christopher Smith/Karl Davies/Ryan Hawley), leaving Jack a widowed single parent. The late 1980s saw two weddings for the Sugdens; first was Jackie to Kathy Bates (Malandra Burrows) and then Joe to Kate Hughes (Sally Knyvette), the latter bringing two teenage children, Mark (Craig McKay) and Rachel (Glenda McKay), to join the family. While Jack had found slow-burning love with librarian Sarah Connolly (Madeleine Howard/Alyson Spiro), he was plagued with tragedy again in 1989 when son Jackie was killed.

Annie married Leonard Kempinski in 1993, but fate struck when a plane crashed on Beckindale, killing both Leonard and young Mark. Jack and Sarah, meanwhile, had happier times when she gave birth to Victoria (Hannah Midgeley/Isabel Hodgins) in 1994, and married later that year. By 1995, Jack was the last original Sugden standing, following Matt and Dolly's departure, Annie's retirement to Spain with new husband Amos, and Joe's untimely death in a car crash.

Annie Sugden

1972–96, 2009 / Played by Sheila Mercier

'When I think of the people I've loved that I've seen go into the ground. Let them go. You'll always have your memories.'
Annie Sugden

Arguably the name most synonymous with *Emmerdale*, Annie encapsulated the gritty, resilient, Yorkshire farmer's wife in every sense of the word: unafraid to speak her mind, and expecting hard work, loyalty and honesty. Family was everything, and strength was what was needed to guide her brood through the most turbulent of times.

During Annie's lifetime she endured the deaths of three husbands, all three of her children, three of her grandchildren, two step-grandchildren, her father and three daughters-in-law. However, it wasn't all doom and gloom, as she had her fair share of suitors during her time in the show. Her eventual third husband, Amos Brearly, proposed in the 70s, as did fellow Woolpack landlord, Henry Wilks. She was courted by Basil Arkroyd and Eddie Hammond, and then an old flame, David Annersley, came out of the woodwork too; but as Annie told Dolly, 'In them days I was as big a romantic as rest of 'em...on t'other hand I'm born and bred a Yorkshire lass and we know the difference between dreams and reality.'

Through it all, Annie was the matriarch of the show, always ready to listen and dish out advice, whether it was wanted or not. Sheila Mercier, who passed away in 2019, aged 100, cut a similar impression off-screen. 'I was terrified of Sheila when I first started. She would sit in the green room very regally,' explains Ian Sharrock. 'I would go on to adore her and realized that she was very shy, and so she could come across as being quite brusque. She was very professional, would always know her lines, always turned up on time.'

Frazer Hines echoes the sentiment: 'The first few days, I thought I couldn't work with Sheila – she was quite snappy. One day she said, "I'm going for a picnic in Roundhay Park, would you like to come?" and I thought I can't be rude and say no, so I went with her, and from that moment on we got on like a house on fire, because I got to know her. Her bark was far worse than her bite.' Frazer adds, 'She'd look at us sternly and we'd think "oh, we'd better behave ourselves". She used to do Sunday lunches, we were like a real family in many ways. She was like a second mother to me.'

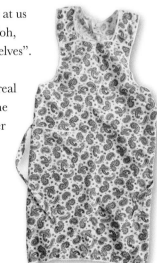

Joe Sugden

1972-83, 1986-94 / Played by Frazer Hines

'I've known Joe since he were a lad – and
I've never met a finer man.'
Amos Brearly

For innate farmer Joe Sugden, considering any other
career was never an option. Having kept the family
farm afloat in the wake of older brother Jack leaving
home, and his father's alcoholism, Joe was a grafter.
One of the original characters of *Emmerdale Farm*,
Joe developed over his time in the show to have
other interests outside of farming. 'As you progress,
the writers see what you're up to in your private life.
I played a lot of charity cricket, so they brought in
cricket matches,' Frazer Hines explains. 'I used to ride
as a jockey, so they brought that in: Joe becomes a
point-to-point rider.'

Frazer's love of horses became a frequent aspect
to Joe's character. 'Joe was going for a ploughing
competition, and we had these two great hulking
Shire horses and I had to drive them up this field.
I had to turn and come back in one shot and the
farmer came up and asked if I'd ploughed before,
and he said, "those are two of the straightest lines I've
ever seen". So I was ploughing, making sure the lines
were straight, and controlling the horses, and doing
my lines.'

Joe was forever waiting for the right woman
in his life, and he had more than his fair share of
romances. 'He had an eye for the ladies and a lot of
love scenes,' Frazer recollects. 'I used to get a lot of
fan letters; in those days you couldn't show a couple
in bed, so Joe used to make love on a rug in front of
his fire and I used to get fan letters asking to borrow
the rug, because it was very lucky, he seemed to get a

lot of women on this rug.' Having finally settled down
with Kate Hughes, she and her teenage children,
Mark and Rachel, provided Joe with the instant family
he'd been missing for so many years.

By 1994, having split from Kate, and with
stepson Mark dying in the plane crash fallout, Joe
hit the bottle, depressed and despondent at life on
the farm, before moving to Spain to join Annie. Joe
died off-screen the following year, Annie bringing his
body back to Emmerdale for burial. Even 50 years
after Joe first appeared on-screen, Frazer's love for his
character remains. 'People used to say, "Frazer, you're
lucky, you're young, and you've got an eye for the
ladies, so there's no acting required" and that's what
I always felt.'

Jack Sugden

1972–73, 1976, 1980–2008 / Played by Andrew Burt /
Clive Hornby

'I love farming this land. I tried to run away from it when
I was younger. Last thing I wanted to be was a farmer. It
drew me back because I'm part of the soil. It was always
going to be my destiny.'
Jack Sugden

The farming legend Jack Sugden who died in 2009
was a far cry from the original black sheep of the
family who returned for his father's funeral in 1972.
At the audience's first introduction to the eldest
Sugden offspring, originally played by Andrew Burt,
Jack was a travelling writer, leading a whimsical and
playboy-like lifestyle, flitting between Rome and
London. Definitely not looking to muck in, and muck
out, at Emmerdale Farm, it would be 1980, and
Clive Hornby taking over the role of Jack, before he
returned as a full-time character. 'Clive immediately
fitted into the slot left by Andrew Burt,' Frazer Hines
recalls. 'He and I were like real brothers, it wasn't all
lovey-dovey, we'd argue sometimes, like real brothers
do, and then we'd make it up and have a few beers.'

Embedding himself into life on the farm, Jack's
importance steadily grew within the show, flying the
flag for the Sugdens, the traditions of the creation
that Kevin Laffan had first imagined, and the rural
farming life (with all its hardships) that *Emmerdale Farm*
was founded on. At the heart of everything, Jack was
a family man, leaving behind a carefree life to settle
with Pat Merrick, then Sarah Connolly, and finally
Diane Blackstock, while living, at various times, with
children Jackie, Robert, Andy and Victoria. 'Victoria
could have been nicer to her dad, I think she could get
away with pushing the boundaries, because her dad

was so amazing,' says Isabel Hodgins. 'Fundamentally
she knew her dad would always be there for her, and
love her unconditionally.'

For many years Jack remained the only original
character still standing in *Emmerdale*, much respected
on- and off-screen, until Clive Hornby's death in
2008. 'Clive and I were golfing buddies, we were
drinking buddies,' Ian Sharrock reflects. 'We'd get
in so much trouble! We had a caravan where we'd
get changed and sit and wait between scenes, and
sometimes it would be rocking with us laughing until
it hurt. I loved him to bits.' Fond memories of Clive
echo across the decades. 'Clive was just wonderful,
he was so funny, he was quite childish with his sense
of humour, which I adored. He had this thing where
we'd be in the green room and a scene would be
called in five minutes and he'd say "oh, best go and
learn it then", every single day, which was a running
joke,' Isabel remembers. 'He loved *Emmerdale* and
working there, so for me, as an absolute beginner, it
was nice to be alongside him.'

Matt & Dolly Skilbeck

1972–89 & 1977–80 (KB); 1980–91 (JR) / Played by Freddie Pyne & Katharine Barker / Jean Rogers

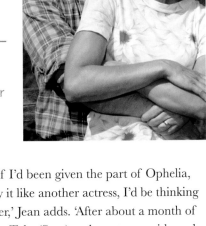

'We're not having rows, that's all in the past, but I feel, I know it's daft, that we're more like friends now, brother or sister even. I feel we can't ever get it back to how it was.'
Dolly Skilbeck

Matt and Dolly Skilbeck were the couple that *Emmerdale Farm* fans rooted for, desperate to see them find happiness. 'Matt was an ordinary Yorkshire country guy, very easy-going, rarely lost his temper, unlike me,' says Freddie Pyne. 'If they were shooting a scene and I thought it wasn't right, I had worked on a farm, so I used to say that if something went out wrong, farmers would complain and I'd get the blame!'

Matt just wanted an easy life, but the 1970s were plagued with misfortune for the shepherd and farmer, who lost his wife and twin toddlers, all in the space of three years. By the end of the decade, things looked up when he was paired with barmaid Dolly Acaster. 'It was Katharine Barker playing Dolly originally,' Freddie explains. 'But she wanted to spend more time with her son, so she left.'

'I was doing a Miss Ellie,' jokes Jean Rogers. 'The only soap really that you'd heard of where one actor took over another part was Miss Ellie in *Dallas*, so YTV were being quite bold. I was up for the role with 50 others.' On-screen, Dolly went away to a convalescent home to recover from a stillbirth, before she returned, now played by Jean. 'I was given the opportunity to look at tapes, so there was all this pressure to try and impersonate Katharine. The way

I looked at it, if I'd been given the part of Ophelia, I wouldn't play it like another actress, I'd be thinking of the character,' Jean adds. 'After about a month of me being there, Toke (Sam) took me to one side and said "Sheila (Annie) thinks you're alright" – any new person coming in she'd give the once over!'

Unfortunately, happiness was short-lived for the Skilbecks, and after their marriage collapsed when Dolly had an affair, Matt left the village. Dolly found herself pregnant by Charlie Aindow, and she opted for an abortion. 'The abortion was a turning point for me. I got some good criticism, but it was hard because of the truth I knew about Dolly,' Jean admits. 'People didn't know why they were disturbed by it, but they were – but Dolly had had a stillbirth and a miscarriage – a difficult time becoming a mother. She was doing it out of strength, not weakness.'

Little is known of Dolly and Matt since their separate moves to Norfolk over 30 years ago. 'I've always thought she'd be in charge of a very nice business,' Jean says. 'Matt would be working as a shepherd on a farm, I don't know whether she and Matt would be still be together.' Freddie adds, 'He's probably given up farming, he'll be in his 80s. I supposed he's happily retired and living in a little thatched cottage in Norfolk somewhere!'

The Sugdens' later years

'My family has fallen apart! I've lost my daughter, Robert hates me, the farm's in ruins,
I have no subsidies and now me herd's gonna be slaughtered!'
Jack Sugden

With Jack, Sarah, Robert and Victoria now set up on
the second incarnation of Emmerdale Farm, after
the first farmhouse gave way to subsidence, they
welcomed waif and stray Andy Hopwood (Kelvin
Fletcher), who was adopted by the Sugdens. In
2000, Sarah and Jack's marriage finally collapsed
after Sarah's affair with lodger Richie Carter, and
Sarah was killed in a barn fire started by Andy.
Diane Blackstock (Elizabeth Estensen) had proved a
loyal friend to Jack, and as the pair grew closer they

planned to marry, but Diane confessed to ex-husband
Rodney that she had cancer, and he helped her
face up to reality. Diane and Jack married and were
thrilled when she was given the all-clear. Meanwhile,
young Andy had fallen in love with Katie Addyman
(Sammy Winward). 'When I got the job, my first
thought was, "Oh my God, how am I going to live up
to the Sugden family",' laughs Sammy Winward. 'But
I just felt really proud to be part of it, to be honest,
and everyone was so welcoming.'

Katie and Andy's marriage ended when Katie had an affair with Robert, a move that ignited a bitter feud between the brothers that led to Jack getting shot and Max King caught the crossfire and then killed in a car crash. Ashamed, Robert left the village. Andy, meanwhile, had fathered a child with Debbie Dingle, with Sarah Sugden Jnr (Sophia Amber Moore/ Katie Hill) providing a link between the two biggest *Emmerdale* families. Andy married Jo Stiles (Roxanne Pallett) in a prison wedding when Andy was finally sent down for Sarah's manslaughter. Released, he struggled to control his temper and would become violent towards Jo until she left, after less than a year of marriage.

In 2009, Sugden patriarch Jack died. His loss was universally mourned, with Annie returning for the funeral and rallying the family. In 2012, Andy would become a father for the second time, when he and Debbie conceived Jack Sugden Jnr (Seth Ball), a saviour sibling to provide Sarah with a bone marrow match.

Robert returned in 2014, by which time Andy had reunited with Katie. Now betrothed to Home Farm heiress Chrissie White (Louise Marwood), Robert married her rather than admit his affair with Aaron Dingle. When Katie discovered the affair and threatened to expose the deceit, Robert pushed Katie through rotten floorboards to her death. Andy took up with Chrissie, but when he had a fling with stepsister Bernice Blackstock, Chrissie fitted him up with father Lawrence's shooting, and he went on the run.

Victoria had meanwhile married Adam Barton (Adam Thomas), but their marriage struggled when Adam discovered he was infertile, and he ultimately went on the run after taking the rap for mum Moira's murder of Emma. Robert finally married Aaron in an official ceremony in 2018, despite having had a one-night stand with Chrissie's sister, Rebecca, and fathering a son, Sebastian, in 2017. Then 2020 saw

Victoria face her toughest challenge when she was raped by Lee Posner, an act that left her pregnant. Victoria gave birth to a much longed-for baby, Harry, while Robert was sent to prison after fatally injuring Lee in an act of revenge.

Following the death of original matriarch Annie in 2020, and the departure of current matriarch Diane in 2021, Victoria is the last Sugden standing. 'When I started, so much of it was in Annie's Cottage, and it was round the table, me, Kelvin and Liz and Clive, it was that family network and it's what it was all about,' Isabel Hodgins recalls. 'So it's bittersweet, because I'm fortunate enough to still be in the show, but the family has accrued many loses. I would like that big family round the table kind of thing again. I guess I'll have to get used to wearing a maternity bump.'

Andy & Katie Sugden

1996–2016 & 2001–15 / Played by Kelvin Fletcher
& Sammy Winward

'You're my best friend, my first love, you know me better than anyone. And bearing that in mind, I can't believe you're giving a plant pot like me a second chance.' **Andy Sugden**

Young Andy Hopwood had a tumultuous start to life and after having started a fire that killed adoptive mum Sarah, guilty Andy became the bane of adoptive brother Robert's life. As Andy hit his teenage years, he met a girl in detention who would change his life: Katie. 'Katie first came in as a bit of a rebel, a bit like Andy, that's probably why they connected early on,' Sammy Winward recalls. 'She wasn't quite as naughty as the years went on, she just made a few mistakes.'

The young star-crossed lovers faced opposition from their fathers when the pair were caught in bed together. Andy and Katie continued to see each other in secret, but when Katie discovered she was pregnant at 15, the families grew to support the couple. Devastation wasn't far round the corner, though, when Katie miscarried. 'She was brought in to do controversial storylines, like the underage sex and miscarrying the baby, so she went through a hell of a lot,' Sammy explains. 'I felt really grateful to be asked to do it, but it was nerve-wracking because you knew there would be people watching who had been through it, so there was that pressure to play it right.'

Andy's brother Robert was never far away from stirring up trouble, and Robert and Katie's affair began, with Andy and Katie even marrying despite her secret infidelity. The affair caused ripples throughout the Sugden family – Victoria discovering the truth and being threatened into mutism by Robert, and Jack getting caught in the crossfire, literally, when Andy went after the pair with a gun.

Andy and Katie split up and took up with other people; Andy with Jo for a time, and Katie with Declan, but it was only ever going to be each other they gravitated towards. 'Katie and Andy got back together, and then I decided that I wanted to move on, so I suppose it did work perfectly, for Andy to be left without Katie,' Sammy muses. Andy and Katie remarried, but Robert meddling in their lives meant til death us do part came sooner than Andy and Katie had thought, when Katie was killed. Andy left not long after, struggling to process Katie's sudden, untimely end. 'It was a special bond. Particularly with childhood sweethearts, there's always that special bond, especially if you stay together, which they did on and off,' Sammy says. 'It sounds cheesy, but it's true love, in its purest of forms.'

Victoria Sugden

1994–Present / Played by Hannah Midgeley / Isabel Hodgins

'I love you Victoria Sugden. I love every beautiful, smart, hilarious bone in your body.'
David Metcalfe

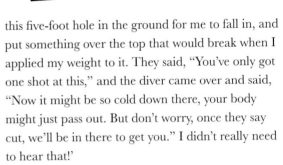

Despite being the core family of *Emmerdale* for over 20 years, these days the Sugdens are an endangered species, saved only by the last woman standing: Victoria. As Annie's only surviving granddaughter, Victoria displays many of the same traits as her grandmother. 'She's very strong, she's got a very clear view of right and wrong and she doesn't mind telling people when they're in the wrong,' reveals Isabel Hodgins. 'She's very family orientated and I like that about her. She's always wanted to be a mum.'

When Victoria gave birth to Harry in 2020, it heralded the end of Victoria's biggest story to date, when, after a night out in 2019, she was followed home and raped by Lee Posner. 'It was tough because I'd put a lot of pressure on myself; I knew it was a big story. It relates to a lot of people, and I think the timing of it, with the Me Too movement, it was a hot topic,' Isabel acknowledges. 'I just wanted to do it well as they were entrusting this story to me. I felt the whole thing was told and handled really well and respectfully. Everyone involved has got a lot to be proud of.'

Victoria is no stranger to trauma, having survived a hole in the heart, a bus crash, a van crashing into a lake, a house fire, a bridge collapse and falling through ice. Isabel recalls filming the 2008 ice stunt. 'It was difficult, but it was so much fun. They created this beautiful winter wonderland set, and there were bits of camera equipment that I'd never seen before,' Isabel explains. 'They'd built

this five-foot hole in the ground for me to fall in, and put something over the top that would break when I applied my weight to it. They said, "You've only got one shot at this," and the diver came over and said, "Now it might be so cold down there, your body might just pass out. But don't worry, once they say cut, we'll be in there to get you." I didn't really need to hear that!'

Starting on *Emmerdale* aged 12, Isabel has spent more of her life on-screen than off. 'Victoria and I have grown up together and I think it's interesting for the audience, because they've watched her turn into this woman.' Taking on a high-profile role at a young age certainly left its impression on Isabel. 'My family always watched the soaps so I knew the character before, so knowing everyone, it makes it much more nerve-wracking,' Isabel confesses. 'I remember leaving one of my auditions and Mark Charnock was walking in, all ten foot of him, and I was like "That's Marlon, and he's a giant!" I was so starstruck!'

The Tates

1989–2005; 2017–Present

'I saw my own father, my dad, the man that I adored, having a fling while my mother was dying of cancer, a fling with Kim, a fling that ultimately cost him his life. And my brother, so consumed with hate, that he tried to take Charity's life away when his own was ending. So self-obsessed that his own little boy, Joseph, counted for nothing.'
Zoe Tate

Tate. The very curt, abrupt nature of the word is a fitting symbol for this no-nonsense stamp upon village life that arrived in late 1989. Fronted by millionaire haulier and self-important patriarch Frank (Norman Bowler), he was joined by his glamorous second wife, Kim (Claire King), his power-hungry son Chris (Peter Amory) and seemingly well-balanced daughter Zoe (Leah Bracknell). The Tates caused ripples, as this nouveau-riche character group looked set to help take the show forward. 'The long-standing cast were happy with where they were, so when we first came in, we were seen as a bit of a disruption, but then we were accepted and everything was fine,' explains Peter Amory. 'I think the fact they were getting away with so much, people hooked onto that. It allowed the writers to write new, different types of stories.'

Despite their ambition, money and power, the Tates took their time to wreak havoc and scandal on the village. 'When we first came in, they were quite a happy, well-balanced family,' says Claire King. 'I think Zoe probably had a little more affection for Kim but Chris couldn't stand her – they were probably going to get together at one point but she thought she'd cut out the middle man and go straight for the head honcho: Frank.'

But this match made in money heaven was doomed. Unfulfilled, Kim sought passion elsewhere, first with Neil Kincaid and then with Dave Glover,

sparking a paternity row when Kim gave birth to James, who proved to be of Tate lineage. Meanwhile, Frank's flaw was drink, his alcoholism helping him on the way to five heart attacks across his time in the Dales.

While Zoe was establishing some independence as a vet, and striking out on her own as the only gay in the village at the time, Chris slithered around the Tate business, waiting to inherit. Chris did prove successful in providing a Tate heir as, having failed in his first marriage to Kathy (Malandra Burrows), Chris sought the comforts of Rachel Hughes (Glenda McKay) following his injuries in the plane crash fallout, which left him unable to walk, and fathered a son, Joseph.

Following Frank's death as a result of Kim's games and manipulation, the Tates' reign at Home Farm came to a temporary end. After Kim became embroiled in a foiled racehorse robbery plot with new husband Steve Marchant (Paul Opacic), she fled from the Dales with baby James.

Chris and Zoe forged on and had to deal with the unexpected appearance of a half-brother, Liam Hammond (Mark Powley), Frank's illegitimate son, who kidnapped Chris and held him hostage. The latest Tate addition was ill-fated, however, when Zoe rescued Chris and shot Liam dead.

After a string of failed romances, Zoe set her sights on Chris's new love interest, Charity Dingle (Emma Atkins). As an unlikely love triangle formed, Charity chose Chris and they married in 2001. The years of trauma finally became too much for Zoe, who developed schizophrenia and was sectioned after burning down the church. In the interim, Zoe had sex with Scott Windsor, conceiving a child, Jean, who was named after her late mother.

Charity, meanwhile, had rekindled her romance with second cousin Cain. Chris discovered the affair and after finding out he was suffering from an inoperable brain tumour, committed suicide, framing

Charity for his murder. Charity was convicted, but after giving birth to Chris's son, Noah, she struck a deal with Zoe – the baby in exchange for her freedom. Charity was released after Zoe changed her testimony, but the courts refused to allow Zoe custody, instead returning him to Charity. Peter Amory considers Chris's response, 'He'd be appalled that Noah is "Dingle", he would not have that,' laughs Peter. 'If Charity and him had split up, that would have been a separate story, he wouldn't want his son called a Dingle!'

After decades of misery in the village, Zoe decided to emigrate to New Zealand, but an attempted murder charge stood in her way – she'd injected Scott with ketamine, fearing he was going to rape her. Zoe was freed when the case collapsed and she left with Joseph and Jean for a new life abroad, pausing only to destroy Home Farm in a gas explosion. The Tates' time in Emmerdale was seemingly up.

FEATURE
THE TATE BUSINESS

Bringing money, security and power, business is the driving force in the Tates' lives. Their portfolio began with Frank Tate & Son Haulage, the company that Frank had built and entrusted son Chris to run. Frank sold the company in 1992, to pay Kim a divorce settlement, but by this point, Frank had bigger plans. Having bought Home Farm Estates in 1989, Frank used the land to build up a sizeable empire, centred around tourism and leisure. Tate Holdings was formed, comprising Home Farm, several tenant farms and cottages in the village, a holiday park of chalets and a swimming pool, fish and game farms, a quarry, a heritage farm and a golf course.

With great fortune came great greed. Kim, whose main interest was always horses – running a livery business and later a stud farm with Lady Tara Oakwell – had enjoyed being in charge during Frank's absences, vying with Chris for power. Writer Bill Lyons recalls, 'I remember watching the early stuff and the look on Claire's face was always "I can do this better than you" and that became the character: she's not Frank's bimbo, she's more intelligent than he is.'

Kim had a controlling share after Frank's death, which continued to cause rivalry between Kim and Chris. 'Chris's role was to just generally stir as much as he could, but Chris would come out the worst,' adds Peter Amory. 'He wanted all of it for himself. His motto would be "it's Tate property, it's Tate business," as long as he could get the name Tate in as much as possible.'

After Kim sold out to Lady Tara, Home Farm slipped from the Tates' grasp. Dejected, Chris started Tate Haulage, which got off to a shaky start after a rivalry with fellow haulier Sean Reynolds, but after a merger, and a cash injection from Zoe, business was on the up.

Zoe, who had always taken a back seat in business, had been content with founding her own veterinary surgery, but she proved herself loyal when she bought back Home Farm and the estate business in 1999, selling it on to Chris in 2001.

Chris founded a subsidiary, Tate Trash, in 2002, and after Chris's death the following year, Zoe gained control of the whole Tate empire, before selling to the Kings in 2005, so she could emigrate to New Zealand.

In 2018, Tom Waterhouse's revelation that he was Joe Tate hailed a new era of Tate business when Joe bought back Home Farm, although Kim's return from prison revealed Joe had been using Kim's money to fund the new empire. Back in control, Kim wasted no time in making her mark: first buying a share in the vets for son Jamie, then investing in the Sharma's burned-out factory, creating Hawsford Outdoor Pursuits (HOP).

'Where were you when her dad was taken away? And all the other times Alice needed a cuddle? When she had toothache? Who's the one who gets her to tidy her room? Tells her off? Kisses her better, makes sure she's got clean socks every day? Who helps her with her homework? And who's the one she comes running to, smiling after school?'
Kathy Glover

Caroline Bates (Diana Davies) had first arrived in the village as Alan Turner's secretary, keeping him in line since 1984, and was joined in 1985 by her children, Kathy (Malandra Burrows) and Nick (Cy Chadwick). While Caroline's stay in Beckindale was cut short in 1989, after ultimately turning down Alan Turner's plans for marriage, her children would remain as permanent figures in the community for nearly 20 years. 'When Cy and I started, we were in the same boat, we were the newbies together. Lovely Di Davies had been in for a while, she took us under her wing,' Malandra remembers. 'It was nice being that little family, but we never thought much of it, because we were told we had three episodes. We were kind of

the guinea pigs, there was no one else that young, we were in our late teens. So it was a really big gamble for *Emmerdale*.'

Kathy would initially find love with husband Jackie Merrick (Ian Sharrock), but in 1989, after only a year of marriage, he was killed in a freak gun accident, shortly after Kathy had miscarried their baby. While Kathy moved on with Chris Tate, Nick got together with Elsa Feldmann. Elsa fell pregnant and gave birth to Alice (Rachel Tolboys). Motherhood proved too restricting for Elsa and she left for city life, Nick took up the role of single parent, moving to Home Farm nursery flat as part of his job. After her marriage to Chris had fallen apart, Kathy embarked on an on-off relationship with Dave Glover. By Christmas 1996, though, Kathy would not only find herself widowed once again, but in sole charge of young Alice, after Nick was sent to prison for ten years, for accidentally shooting dead a poacher.

Kathy would continue to raise Alice, all the while running her diner and batting off failed relationships with Biff Fowler and Graham Clark, until 1999, when Alice left to join Elsa, now settled in Australia. Kathy herself would pack up and join Alice and Elsa in 2001. Off-screen, Kathy would finally find stable happiness and give birth to her own baby girl in 2002, then would make a brief appearance in 2005, returning for Seth Armstrong's funeral.

'What's God got against the Glover family?'
Jan Glover

Ned and Jan Glover thought everything would be all right moving to Holdgate Farm in 1995, but fast-forward three years and their marriage was in tatters and two of their three children dead. The hardworking farming family first arrived in Emmerdale in 1994, living out of a caravan Ned had won in a fight. A stubborn, very traditional family man Ned (Johnny Leeze) and his loyal wife Jan (Roberta Kerr) had raised three very grounded children in Our Dave (Ian Kelsey), Our Linda (Tonicha Jeronimo) and Our Roy (Nicky Evans). The Glovers struggled with money problems, their daughter Linda's unplanned pregnancy that she tried to terminate herself, nearly dying in the process, and Dave's affair with lady of the manor, Kim Tate, despite being married to Kathy. 'So many people laughed at Kathy and Dave. It didn't last very long, because simmering in the background was Kim on the warpath, and the viewers could see what was going to

happen,' Malandra recalls. 'And lots of people were devastated by that, especially with the departure of lovely Ian Kelsey.' His attraction to Kim proved fatal when he died saving her baby. For a while the Glovers thought, and hoped, that Kim's baby, James, was Dave's, but DNA tests proved otherwise. Less than a year later, after Linda had finally married sweetheart Biff Fowler (Stuart Wade), she was also killed in a car crash. Poor Jan, so consumed with grief, kidnapped baby James, leading to her being sectioned. Jan struggled to readjust afterwards and left Ned to live with her sister.

Ned jetted off for a new life running a bar in Ibiza in 1999, leaving Roy at the mercy of Kelly Windsor, who'd finally come round to the idea of marriage. The newlyweds' relationship was brief, however, when Roy followed Ned to Ibiza in 2000.

Kathy Glover

1985–2001, 2005 / Played by Malandra Burrows

'If anyone was ever due any good luck it's Kathy.'
Jack Sugden

When young Kathy Bates first arrived in Beckindale, little did she know of the trials and tribulations that village life had in store for her. Immersing herself in rural life, Kathy ditched A-level studies for farm work – first at Home Farm, then Emmerdale Farm – all adding to her varied CV that, over the years, would boast poultry farm worker, abattoir attendant, farm shop worker, stable girl, barmaid, HGV driver and tearooms owner.

It was her work at Emmerdale Farm that would seal her first village romance and later marriage to Jackie Merrick. The union only lasted a year when Jackie was killed, and so began Kathy's misfortune with relationships. 'Everyone blames Kathy – every man you marry, something happens,' Malandra Burrows laughs. 'Every time an actor was going to leave, they paired them with Kathy. They'd say, Malandra, we love the way you cry, so we'll marry them off and then the husband will have another sad end!' After Jackie, Kathy went on to marry Chris Tate, but when the marriage was blighted with affairs, and struggling to adapt to Chris's disability, the relationship fell apart. 'Peter Amory was great to work with, and work against. We had so many great rows, it gave the writers so much, but we had to learn ten-page rows, so it took some doing,' Malandra recalls.

Kathy moved on with estate manager Dave Glover, but Dave only had eyes for Kim Tate, ensuring Kathy was left widowed once again when he died saving Kim's baby. Kathy took a trip down the aisle again in 1999, with Biff Fowler, but they never made it through the vows, while her dalliance with psycho Graham Clark nearly cost Kathy her life. The clifftop showdown, leading to Graham's demise, left Kathy hanging on, literally, and Kathy lost another of her nine lives. Seemingly indestructible, Kathy's time in the village saw her survive a miscarriage, being run over by a horsebox, stuck in a car dangling over a cliff, and a lorry crashing into the bus she was on.

Kathy's constant through it all, however, was her beloved niece, Alice, who Kathy cared for after her brother, Nick, went to prison. 'Rachel (Alice) was with us from a little two-year-old, and was absolutely amazing,' Malandra explains. 'You're always taught never to work with animals or children – and I ended up on *Emmerdale* working with both!' Kathy left to join Alice in Australia in 2001 and now reportedly has a husband and child. 'I didn't know Kathy had a daughter!' Malandra laughs. 'Betty mentioned it, that she'd had a letter from Kathy, so I thought, really, when did this happen?!'

Biff & Linda Fowler

1994-99, 2005 & 1994-97 / Played by Stuart Wade & Tonicha Jeronimo

'I don't think I've seen a couple more in love than you two.'
Dave Glover

One of the most wholesome relationships in *Emmerdale*'s history was that of young lovers Biff and Linda. While Linda Glover first arrived as the only daughter of farming grafters Ned and Jan, Biff was more of a waif and stray, tiring of his mother's relationship with her abusive partner, and escaping to rent a room from Seth and Betty Armstrong. As Biff became a surrogate son to the old couple, he embarked on a romance with Jessica McAllister, his friend Luke's sister, and landed a job at Home Farm, working alongside mate Dave Glover. Vets' receptionist Linda, meanwhile, was the good girl led astray by arrogant toff Danny Weir, who strung her along and left her pregnant while he became engaged to someone more of his social standing. Mortified, Linda terminated the pregnancy herself, using drugs from the vets' surgery, an act that nearly cost her life. When her father Ned angrily confronted Danny at his family mansion and tried to drown him in his own swimming pool, kindhearted Biff, who'd been sweet on Linda, stepped up to support her.

Everyone rooted for the young lovers, who were determined to do things properly, set themselves up in their own place and wait until marriage before sleeping together. 'They were fabulous. I thought Biff was a superb character,' Malandra Burrows recalls. 'I loved Biff and Linda, because they came from similar backgrounds.' Their much-anticipated wedding on Christmas Eve 1996 was a huge family, and village, affair, but it was marred by the death of Linda's brother Dave, as he saved baby James Tate from a fire that night.

The death seemed to cast a cloud over the Fowlers' marriage, as money woes meant they had to leave their little cottage and move in with Linda's parents, while Biff reunited with his father on his deathbed and was devastated to learn that he had inherited his dad's Huntington's disease gene. Worried about the future of the children that he and Linda planned, Biff struggled with the revelation, particularly when Linda fell pregnant, only to miscarry.

The Fowlers' marriage came to an abrupt halt when, after a row at a party, Linda went speeding off with coked-up Lord Alex Oakwell, only for him to crash the car and kill Linda. Young widower Biff tried to forge a new life on his own, taking up first with Kelly Windsor, then as posh Lady Tara's bit of rough, and then with Kathy Glover, only for their marriage not to make it past the wedding service. Biff escaped Emmerdale on his beloved motorbike.

The Windsors & Hopes

1993–Present

'You honestly think we want to spend another minute with you and that scumbag son of yours?'
'He's your brother.'
'The only one I care about is Donna. I pity her because she's stuck with you.'
Kelly & Viv Windsor

(Sophie Jefferey/Verity Rushworth). 'The kids were great. I loved Toby, he looked so like me. And Adele, we still keep in contact, she had Alun's frame of face, and my eyes, but then we found out she wasn't my daughter, she was my stepdaughter!' Deena recalls. 'We were all very into musicals, so between takes, when they were setting up, I taught my girls, we'd all be dancing and singing. Especially when Verity came in, when she was about 12, and Ben as well, we all got on really well, and we'd always get told off. And then Verity went off to musicals, and her first West End musical was in Shaftesbury, where I did my first.'

Despite the name, the Windsor family were anything but regal, first landing in Beckindale in 1993. With village life a far cry from the fast pace of London, the family struggled to adapt at first, leaving gates open and causing wildlife to escape, and screaming round the lanes in their trademark white Zephyr. For parents Vic (Alun Lewis) and Viv (Deena Payne), it was their second go at marriage, with Vic having lost his wife Anne, leaving him to raise their daughter Kelly (Adele Silva), and Viv divorced from convict husband Reg, leaving her to raise Scott (Toby Cockerell/Ben Freeman). Vic and Viv had married and had Donna

'All those offspring…busy boy, our Bob!'
Pearl Ladderbanks

Despite the fresh new start for the blended family, it wasn't long before Viv gave in to temptation with her dance partner, Vic's mate, Terry Woods. Vic and Viv separated for a time, and while they reconciled, things would never be the same. Vic was killed on Christmas Day 1998, by injuries sustained in the post office robbery by Billy Hopwood. Viv struggled to hold the family together, with Kelly and Scott proving the most troublesome when the step-siblings embarked on an affair. Kelly fell pregnant, unsure if the baby was Scott's or new husband Roy Glover's (Nicky Evans). Kelly lost the baby after a suicide attempt, and despite planning a new life with Roy in Ibiza, he ditched her when he finally had enough of her games.

Viv's fortunes turned around when she met travelling salesman Bob Hope (Tony Audenshaw). Relighting Viv's romantic fire, the two got together, and despite Kelly making a play for him, Bob and Viv married in 2001. However, Bob came with baggage: four failed marriages and five kids: Dawn, Jamie, Josh, Carly and Roxy, two of which, Dawn (Julia Mallam)

and Jamie (Alex Carter), would join Bob in the village. 'You feel an affinity to those characters and people as you're like a father figure in a way,' Tony explains.

Bob was horrified when eldest, Dawn, shacked up with his mate, Terry, and married him after discovering she was pregnant. Dawn gave birth to Terry Junior 'TJ', in 2003, but the day after the birth, Terry, while celebrating in the pub, suffered a debilitating stroke. Scott, meanwhile, had had a fling with Zoe Tate, despite his homophobic abuse towards her when he was a teenager. Their dalliance would produce a child, Jean Jnr, in 2003.

'The truth is, I'm not a very good grandad,
am I? Or dad come to that. I've got kids
littered all over the place.'
Bob Hope

Viv and Bob split up in 2005, when she had
an affair with Paddy Kirk, but they reunited and
remarried in 2006, in a double ceremony with Donna
and Marlon. The same year also saw the untimely
death of Dawn, a victim of the Kings' treacherous
house collapse, which left Bob and Jamie baying
for blood, and suspects in Tom King's murder. On
the day of Dawn's funeral, Viv discovered she was
pregnant, and she and Bob were stunned to find out
she was expecting twins. Cathy (Gabrielle Dowling)
and Heath (Sebastian Dowling) were born in early
2007, on the moors.

The year 2008 saw Viv face a stretch in
prison, having been framed for a charity money
embezzlement. In her absence, Bob allowed Brenda
Walker (Lesley Dunlop) to buy into the Hopes' café
and shop business, while he embarked on a fling with
her adoptive daughter, Gennie. When Viv came

out of prison, enraged at the deceit, she separated
from Bob.

Viv served her last customer in 2011 when she
fell victim to DS Nick Henshall's hero syndrome and
the fire he started spread to the shop flat, killing her
and Terry, who'd tried to rescue her. Bob was left in
charge of the infant twins, and with Brenda, rebuilt
the business into a café. Kelly made a return the same
year, dropping the bombshell on Jimmy King that
he had fathered a child with her, young Elliot (Luca
Hoyle), while half-sister Donna did the same thing
in 2014, returning to reveal to ex-husband Marlon
that she'd secretly had his daughter, April (Amelia
Flanagan) five years previously.

Bob's own daughter Carly (Rebecca Ryan /
Gemma Atkinson) would join the family in 2015,
leading Bob to commit fraud to try to help her out
with money, which resulted in a spell in prison for him.
Carly came with her own tragic secret, too – she'd
previously lost a baby, Billy, to cot death. After a brief
relationship with Marlon, Carly would leave to reunite
with Billy's dad. Bob and Brenda, who'd been together
since 2013, made things official in
2018, but the marriage was over by
the reception, after his ill-fated
affair with Laurel Thomas.
Brenda and Bob now co-parent
teenage Cathy and Heath, while
Brenda is with Eric Pollard, and
Bob with Wendy Posner. 'A while
ago it was quite a dynasty and
that has been eroded a bit and
I've got a much smaller family,'
laughs Tony.

Viv Hope

1993-2011 / Played by Deena Payne

'You really are a very sexy woman, Viv.'
Bob Hope

Petite and feisty, postmistress Viv Hope was the font of all village gossip, looking down on everyone with a disapproving glare from behind her shop counter. However, Viv's dominant presence did not happen overnight. 'When I first arrived, I really didn't have much of a clue,' Deena Payne admits. 'I was used to being directed and told, this is the character, but in a soap, you have to bring the character with you, because the directors only work on so many episodes.'

The biggest morph to her character was following Vic's death, when Deena effected change. 'I felt she could be a bit more of a gossip, be a bit stronger. I loved the padded shoulders in the 70s and 80s, and I thought, my pins are alright, so short, tight skirts and heels,' Deena recalls. 'I thought 60s hair, and I really like it when it's backcombed, and then I went into wardrobe and suggested bright colours: yellows, greens. I just thought, "go over the top girl", mutton dressed as lamb!'

A busybody, Viv would frequently get people's backs up with her nosiness and judgements, which Deena relished. 'There's a side of me and my personality that I really didn't want anyone else to see, that I exorcized through Viv. She often spoke before she thought what she said, and that used to get her into trouble,' Deena adds. 'She was a very caring mother, but she hardened up to everyone else, because she'd been through a lot.'

Having endured a rotten first marriage to criminal Reg Dawson, and then a second marriage cut short when Vic died, Viv finally found happiness with Bob Hope, although Deena's first impressions weren't as great. 'In the auditions there were six blokes auditioning for Bob, when Tony did his, there was something about him I didn't like, I don't know what it was!' Deena muses. 'But then in retrospect he looked like a male version of Viv. And the way he played Bob was kind of slapstick, whereas Viv was very serious, but in doing that, it was quite funny. I really enjoyed working with him, we kind of gelled.'

Despite being killed off in 2011, Deena has not given up hope, literally, for Viv's return one day. 'I'm not in the graveyard. I was really hurt about that. But you haven't seen my body. I'm still in the forest, in the woods,' Deena jokes. 'Terry's there too, with a really long beard. We're jiving away, eating the grass. She could walk into The Woolpack in a very short cream skirt and cream wings!'

Kelly Windsor

1993–2000, 2005–7, 2011 / Played by Adele Silva

'You're a nasty piece of work, Kelly Windsor.'
Viv Hope

Kelly Windsor started off as the spoilt daughter, but as she grew into her teenage years, she emerged from a troubled girl to a minx with an agenda: men and money. Part of the blended Windsor family, Kelly got on well with half-sister Donna, but had few other allies, having fallen for stepbrother Scott, lost her father and never seeing eye to eye with stepmother Viv. 'It was a fractious relationship between Kelly and Viv, they were both quite vibrant personalities, and they clashed,' Deena Payne explains. 'Kelly was her father's daughter, and when he went, she started to go off the rails a bit. Viv was a tart with a heart and that rubbed off on Kelly – but she was more tart than heart!'

Kelly remained tethered to her family, relying on them when she had nowhere else to go, but she had a penchant for choosing inappropriate male suitors, or treating them like dirt when she did find someone kind and reliable. Teenage Kelly went out with Will Cairns, before starting a relationship with her teacher, Tom Bainbridge, who was sacked when the school found out. Kelly slept with Biff, by whom she became pregnant, only to lose the baby, and then with Chris Tate, as well as her own stepbrother, Scott. She married kind-hearted Roy Glover, but constantly miserable and whining, Kelly was never satisfied with stick-in-the-mud Roy. After her marriage to Roy fell apart, Kelly tried it on with Viv's new man, Bob Hope, before leaving the village in shame. 'I remember having a scene where I had to give her a right-hander, and she had to slap me back,' Deena

recalls. 'And the director said hit her and I bloody did and she hit me back!'

Kelly returned a few years later, again making a play for anything in trousers – particularly expensive ones – and set up with sugar daddy Rodney Blackstock, before turning her attentions to Jimmy King. Pregnant with his baby, she opted for an abortion, which Jimmy discovered on their wedding day. Rather than face the music, Kelly roared out of Emmerdale in a Porsche stolen from Debbie Dingle. In a spectacular return several years later, she gave Jimmy the news that she had given birth to his son, Elliot. Arguing, she whacked Jimmy round the head, causing amnesia, which she tried to capitalize on by making out they were together. Jimmy fell for her ploy, until his memory returned and Kelly was run out of the village once again. She is now living the high life in LA.

Bob Hope

2000–Present / Played by Tony Audenshaw

'I have made an unholy cock-up of my life. Two kids in Spain: I've only just started seeing Carly and Josh again, I tell me boss I'm staying with Mrs Mac so I can claim expenses while I sleep in a field, it's hardly an edifying tale.'
Bob Hope

As barman at The Woolpack, and server in the café, happy-go-lucky Bob Hope enjoys bringing a smile to people's faces. Always with a twinkle in his eye, his roots as a lingerie salesman for 'Naughty Nylons' are clear with his chirpy chat and cheeky banter. 'I've got the original breakdown for the character. He was sort of described as quite a gregarious salesman,' Tony Audenshaw explains. 'He's a happy-go-lucky character, he likes a good time, bit of an everyman.' Brought into *Emmerdale* as a new love interest for postmistress Viv, producers were unsure of how this new lothario would be received. 'I was brought in for three months, and they weren't sure whether that relationship with Viv would work. But thankfully it was something they developed, and I was very grateful for that,' says Tony.

Quickly established as the new man in Viv's life, Bob would go on to marry, divorce, and then remarry Viv, creating one of the show's most convivial couples. 'It was great working with Deena. We had a lot of lines, a lot of words, with a lot of fast patter,' Tony recalls. 'They were such great characters to play, we were very affectionate to each other. We worked with director Ian Bevitt, and he really encouraged gilding the scripts a bit with what we called each other. So we went very lovey-dovey – "yes my little munchkin" was one, and that was a key part of the relationship.' Hopeless romantic Bob hasn't had a great deal of

luck when it comes to his marriages and family life. Married seven times, to five different women, and with seven children, Bob has left a trail of broken hearts and dysfunctional family life in his wake. 'He's got a history of not hanging around when he's had problems within a marriage,' Tony adds. 'He's flitted and moved on. He ran away from his problems and pretended they didn't happen. He does like to be around his family, whatever family that is at the time. He loves a wedding!'

Despite Bob's rollercoasters, Tony shows no sign of tiring of his alter ego. 'He's a likeable character on the whole, and a fun personality, which is always good if you're going to be in a soap for a long time. Sometimes it gets serious, sometimes hyper-comedic, and I'm part of both. He's a great gift to play.'

The Dingles

1994–Present

'The Dingles dynasty. We're what you might call Yorkshire's answer to...'
'The Kennedys?'
'I don't think I'd pass for Jackie.'
Zak, Mandy & Lisa Dingle

The Dingles: where 'keep it in the family' can mean anything from not grassing on your own, to marrying your cousin. Soap's biggest, loudest, most garish family first crashed onto TV screens in 1994, consisting of village outcasts – former bare-knuckle fighter Zak Dingle (Steve Halliwell) and Nellie Dingle (Sandra Gough/Maggie Tagney), and their grown-up children Butch (Paul Loughran), Ben (Steve Fury), Sam (James Hooton) and Tina (Jacqueline Pirie). Dozens of Dingles, across five generations, have appeared through the years; some have stuck around and made a lasting mark on village life, some have passed through with brief chaos, others have only been referred to. Their family tree can be traced back generations and boasts various 'clans' from the 'Irish'

Dingles to the 'Southampton' Dingles, to Guiseppe Dingle in Italy, and Crocodile Dingle in Australia.

'The Dingles are like a sub-class, no one feels inferior to the Dingles, we don't intimidate anyone socially,' Mark Charnock believes. 'There's a lot of comedy in the family, people like that, and when something serious happens to them the Dingles all lock together.' Lucy Pargeter adds, 'If you put all the Dingles in a police line-up, you could name us all and I think that's genius. They know who the Dingles are. That's all about the look, like Zak with the cap, we've all got our little trademarks.'

'We're still a family, no matter who tries to threaten us or split us apart. Nothing can break us. Not death, nor any other scum. We are Dingles.'
Nellie Dingle

Ben Dingle, the first Dingle to appear on-screen, was killed in 1994, leading to a feud with the McAllisters, whose son Luke the family blamed for Ben's death. This led to Tina's ill-fated revenge plan against Luke, ending in his tragic death. Tina fled to London in 1996, and after Nellie left the family for Ireland, the lady of the Dingle homestead was cousin Mandy (Lisa Riley), before Zak got together with Lisa Clegg (Jane Cox). Cousin Marlon (Mark Charnock) joined the clan in 1996, arriving with his ex-con father, Albert (Bobby Knutt), who was always looking for the next scam. Enterprising Mandy hoped to strike gold when she converted an old caravan to a food shack, Mandy's Munchbox, sparking a Dingles war with a rival trailer, which ended when the Munchbox was blown up.

Zak and Lisa had a surprise Christmas present in 1998 – baby Belle (Eden Taylor-Draper), born in the pigsty. Meanwhile, both Emily Wylie (Kate McGregor) and Paddy Kirk (Dominic Brunt) joined the family in 1999, when Emily took up with Butch, and Paddy finally married Mandy – who'd annulled her marriage of convenience to cousin Butch. Following Butch's untimely death in 2000, just after his deathbed wedding to Emily, the Dingle clan expanded, with the arrival of Zak's brother Shadrach (Andy Devine), his son Cain (Jeff Hordley) and second

cousin Charity (Emma Atkins), who arrived for the funeral. While Charity made a play for rich Chris Tate, Shadrach's ex-wife Faith (Gillian Jephcott/Sally Dexter) had a surprise of her own for Zak – he, not Shadrach, was Cain's father. Cain's sister, Chas (Lucy Pargeter), would follow him to Emmerdale in 2002, arriving as a stripper in a nun's outfit. Meanwhile, Zak went on a trail for the lost Dingle fortune in Chile, after reconciling with his dying father Jedediah (Richard Mayes), having wrongly believed his mother Peg (Jeanne Hepple) had killed him decades before.

Marlon found happiness with Tricia Stokes (Sheree Murphy), marrying her in 2003, only to find himself a widower a year later, while Charity fought for freedom, having been framed by Chris for his own death. Charity and Cain had had an affair, drawn together by the arrival of long-lost daughter Debbie (Charley Webb). Charity sold baby Noah (Jack Downham) in exchange for her freedom, only to be reunited with him when the courts refused his aunt Zoe custody. The introduction of 11 new, temporary Dingles followed in 2004: Solomon (Paul Shane), Zak's cousin, as well as Elvis, Marilyn, Lilith, Matthew, Mark, Luke, Jon, Mystic, Brando and Daniel. Solomon fought Zak for title of King Dingle, which Solomon won by cheating. After failing to cause a split in the Dingle family, Solomon left, defeated.

A whole new Dingle generation began in 2005 when young Debbie gave birth to Sarah (Sophia Amber Moore/Katie Hill), while cousin Delilah (Hayley Tamaddon) arrived, escaping from her own wedding. The following year was an eventful one for the Dingles, when Sam married terminally ill Alice (Ursula Holden-Gill), having had baby Samson (Sam Hall) with her, before she died. Marlon tried a second bash at marriage, with Donna Windsor (Verity Rushworth), while his troublesome brother Eli (Joe Gilgun) arrived. Eli's presence in Marlon's life would nearly prove fatal in 2007, when he 'helped' Marlon to recoup some winnings from a bookie with the aid of a gun. Marlon ended up getting shot and as he survived the injuries, he was hailed a hero for intervening in the robbery, angering Eli. In 2008, Emmerdale saw the permanent arrival of Aaron (Danny Webb/Danny Miller) at mother Chas's door, after several fleeting visits in the past, while Chas had to deal with another skeleton in the closet with the revelation she had a half-sister, Genesis (Sian Reese-Williams), by Shadrach. The following year, Charity, Noah and Cain all made permanent returns to the homestead. Alcoholic waster Shadrach finally paid the price for his drinking in 2010 when a liver condition saw him collapse in the river and drown, despite Marlon trying to save him. The Dingles commemorated Shadrach's life as they knew best – by burying him in their back garden!

Meanwhile, Eli made an escape from the village as, after falling out with Sam over their attraction to illegal immigrant Olena Petrovich, Eli had attacked Eric Pollard during a robbery. He managed to get accused Sam off the hook by confessing, before fleeing.

Marlon finally achieved his dream of becoming a father in 2011, when former lover Rhona Goskirk gave birth to Leo (Harry Whittaker/Harvey Rogerson), and Cain became a reluctant father again, having got teenager Amy Wyatt pregnant with son Kyle Winchester (Huey Quinn). The next two years saw the Dingle family grow yet again, with the marriages of Charity to Jai, Chas to Dan, and Gennie to Nikhil, as well as the births of Jack (Seth Ball) to Debbie and Andy, and Molly (Maia Rose Smith) to Gennie and Nikhil. Gennie's happiness would be short-lived, though, as she fell foul to Debbie's serial-killer boyfriend, Cameron Murray.

'Dingle's not just a name, it's a reputation.'
Mandy Dingle

Yet more Dingle wedding bells chimed in 2014, with Cain and Moira (Natalie J Robb), Marlon and Laurel (Charlotte Bellamy) and Charity and Declan (Jason Merrells) all marrying. Meanwhile, the return of Marlon's ex, Donna, threw up a revelation in the shape of their secret daughter, April (Amelia Flanagan). Marlon was left to raise April himself when terminally ill Donna committed suicide.

Debbie's marriage to Pete Barton (Anthony Quinlan) was over by the reception in 2015, and Charity gave birth to Moses (Arthur Cockroft) while in prison – taking over a share of The Woolpack, alongside second cousin Chas, upon her release. Patriarch Zak's marriage to Lisa ended abruptly following the revelation of his affair with family friend Joanie Wright (Denise Black), but their relationship was brief when, after marrying her, Zak realized he'd made a mistake. After Joanie died suddenly, Zak was desperate to reunite with Lisa, and they tentatively tried again.

Bad penny Faith made a return in 2017, while Cain and Moira reunited after a separation, following the birth of their son, Isaac (Bobby Dunsmuir). Charity's long-lost son Ryan (James Moore) became the latest addition to the family in 2018, while Aaron finally married Robert, and Chas, now with Paddy, endured the birth and death of baby Grace. Mandy made a surprise return to the Dales the following year, with stepson Vinny (Bradley Johnson) in tow, arriving for the wedding of Marlon to fourth wife Jessie (Sandra Marvin). Zak and Lisa tried to make a go of it again by remarrying, but Lisa, who knew she was dying, passed away after the reception. Brighter times were ahead for Paddy and Chas, as they had a baby girl, Eve (Billy and Bonnie Clement), then married at the end of 2020. Sam and Lydia (Karen Blick) also wed earlier in the year. Meanwhile, Cain was rocked by the arrival of his unknown son of almost 30 years, Nate (Jurell Carter). 'Initially, because he came between family members, it turned people's noses up and made people not want to have anything to do with him,' Jurell Carter explains. 'But as time's gone on, one by one, with Cain last, they've realized that inside he's still a little boy who's longing for his father.' Nate made Cain a grandfather again in 2021, when his partner Tracy Metcalfe gave birth to baby Frankie.

'I'm so pleased to call myself a Dingle,' says James Hooton. 'There's Dingles of all shapes, sizes, virtues, abilities, it is the family.' Mark Charnock adds, 'It's such a mixed bag of characters as well. To have someone who's tough and cool like Cain, and someone as earthy and funny as Zak, and as wily and irreverent as Chas, somebody crazy like Charity, someone as sweet as Belle. We're a great patchwork.'

Zak & Lisa Dingle

1994–Present & 1996–2019 / Played by Steve Halliwell & Jane Cox

'You stole my heart, Lisa Dingle. For ever and all time.' **Zak Dingle**

The undisputed head of the whole Dingle clan, Zak was the rough and always ready for a fight leader of the sprawling, uncouth and unsavoury Dingle pack from the off. A much-detested family living on the outskirts of the village, the Dingles gradually bedded into the landscape, with Zak's temper and fearsome grip on his children easing following the break-up of his marriage to matriarch Nellie, and the loss of two of his sons, Ben and Butch.

'Zak is my favourite character, because Steve has always played him as a rogue, but also loveable,' Peter Amory explains. 'I love how Steve didn't make him a total idiot. There's a lot of comedy in him.' A loveable rogue to villagers and viewers, Zak soon won the affections of local pig farmer-turned-mechanic, Lisa Clegg. The absolute equal to Zak, the chemistry was unrivalled, their bond strong and their dedication to each other indisputable. Lisa proved herself a worthy Dingle matriarch, taking on the family with gusto and love, steering the Dingles through crisis after crisis, and putting any of them, including Zak, in their place when needed. 'They're the greatest Dingle couple ever,' says Lisa Riley. 'They're soap legends. And every generation will know about Zak and Lisa.'

Having married and had their own daughter, Belle, together, Zak and Lisa seemed solid as a rock, weathering such dark times as Zak's testicular cancer and Lisa's rape by colleague Derek Benrose. But even the toughest partnerships can reach their breaking point, and Zak and Lisa's came when Zak did the unthinkable and went off with another woman – his affair with friend Joanie exposed by Belle over Christmas dinner in 2015.

Zak and Lisa split, much to the devastation of their family, and spent a year apart before Lisa tentatively allowed herself to reconcile with Zak. However, living a long and reunited old age wasn't to be for the Dingle couple, and on the day they remarried, Lisa passed away after the reception, leaving Zak bereft.

On-screen daughter Belle, actor Eden Taylor-Draper, feels just as close off-screen as on-screen to her television parents, 'They are the ultimate couple, and they are like my second parents. Whenever we write birthday cards and stuff they put "from Dad/from Mum". I adore them both so much. They've just been amazing to be around and to grow up with.'

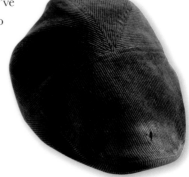

Sam Dingle

1995–98, 2000–Present / Played by James Hooton

'Take Sam, he's neither use nor ornament that lad, and as thick as two short planks. And he's the nicest of the bunch.' **Viv Hope**

One of the original Dingle family, Sam was the runt of Zak and Nellie's litter – not streetwise or savvy, and always in trouble with the law. 'He's been referred to several times as a "bit thick", "not all there", "a little bit special", "slow",' lists James Hooton. 'He's not the sharpest knife in the drawer, and he potentially had learning difficulties growing up.' The subject of pity, or derision, by those around him, Sam found a guiding hand in the shape of conman Eric Pollard. Sam grew independence from the family by working for, some would say being exploited by, Pollard, who used Sam as a general dogsbody and fall guy for his burgeoning antiques business. The Artful Dodger to Pollard's Fagin, Sam was always keen to impress Mr P, and over the years Pollard has grown genuinely to support Sam – such as helping him to do a reading at brother Butch's funeral, after Kathy taught him to read.

'He's certainly grown up, and I've grown up with him from my early 20s. He's written for differently now, and that's the most realistic part of the change of any character, how they're written for in a show such as this,' explains James. As Sam found love with Alice Wilson, he found himself thrust into maturity, having to care for their newborn son, Samson. 'As he's got older, he's got more responsibility. He had to deal with being a parent, then his wife getting non-Hodgkin's lymphoma, and then deal with her euthanasia request,' James adds. 'I think that's part of his coming of age and growing up. Like most long-

serving characters on a soap, he's experienced things that have changed him.'

Having just found love with Alice before she was cruelly snatched away, it would be years before Sam found his equal again, with Lydia Hart. As Sam settled down with her, it was clear there was room in his heart for both of his beloved wives. 'I was talking to Carol, one of the costume ladies, before Sam and Lydia's wedding and we were talking about a watershed moment where Sam gives his wedding ring to his son, as a keepsake,' James recalls. 'It's the final goodbye to his wife that's passed away. He loved her equally as much as he does Lydia.'

As Sam continues to step up to the fold and become an important part of the Dingle family, his popularity never wavers. 'Sam Dingle's my favourite character,' says Eden Taylor-Draper. 'He ticks every box, he can be hilarious, but then his story with Alice was heartbreaking. He's an all-round character.' With dad Zak getting older, Sam has begun to take up the mantle of head of the Dingle homestead. 'He's a good soul, he'll do anything for his family,' James adds. 'He's one of the *Emmerdale* good guys.'

Mandy Dingle

1995–2001, 2019–Present / Played by Lisa Riley

'Big Mandy, good for a laugh. She's always so strong
– nothing gets to her. Always a joke, always a laugh.'
Mandy Dingle

Bold and brash, Mandy is an explosion of fun, colour
and cheer that first appeared as a Dingle family
member at Tina and Luke's wedding. 'Mandy was
only supposed to be in one episode, but the writers
saw that there was something special there,' Lisa Riley
explains. 'Then I went to Palma on holiday, and my
mum faxed the hotel to say my agent was trying to
get hold of me! The response to that one episode had
been so incredible and Mervyn Watson (Producer)
said, "I don't know what you've done Lisa, but the
audience have really grasped this character." So six
months turned to seven and a half years!'

Never afraid to take anyone on, Mandy has
been hurt countless times over the years, usually by
affairs of the heart – her courtship and later marriage
to Paddy was rocky, particularly as his mother
disapproved, and her relationship with Paul was
blighted by his secret gambling and physical abuse
of son Vinny. 'Mandy's got the biggest heart. She
oozes loyalty. It's family all the way. She loves who she
loves and she loathes who she loathes,' Lisa adds.
'We always say with Mandy it's like a piano, there's
the left-hand low key and then the top one, and no
others in between.'

After her marriage to Paddy collapsed, Mandy
left in 2001. After many calls for Lisa to bring Mandy
back to screen, she eventually agreed nearly 20 years
later. 'It was initially really hard, the whole format
of the show was different, the volume of episodes,
and the new writers had to find her voice again, but

we got there quite fast,' says Lisa. With Mandy back
where she belongs, the character's spark has never
been brighter, with the laughs harder and the sadness
stronger. 'It's just a joy playing Mandy, I love making
people cry and laugh and the writers are just great
with that. She's not a doormat, she has a real deep-
rooted vulnerability, as so many woman do, and
Mandy's not afraid to show it,' Lisa acknowledges.
'Karin Young wrote me the most beautiful line:
"Relationships and businesses, I've got all the right
ideas, I just keep making mistakes." I love that you
get to see this real person.'

In terms of getting into character, Mandy is
worlds away from Lisa, who is methodical in her
approach to Mandy. 'I always say that when I go to
work and I put the wig on, the lashes on, the makeup
on, I'm not like that at all, it's the best trunk to open,
the Mandy trunk. You never have a boring day
playing Mandy Dingle.'

FEATURE
DINGLE COURT

'It's not like some social club where you can just come and go as you like. We have our own rules.'
Zak Dingle

A Dingle Court can be called for by any Dingle. All available Dingles assemble, and the Dingle Judge, Zak, or in his absence Cain or Sam, presides with the Dingle Bible in front of them and the Dingle Judicial Ladle in hand. If done properly, the Judge appoints someone to put forward a prosecution case, and someone for a defence. Everyone has their say, and then the family vote, usually on whether the accused should be allowed to remain or should be exiled from the family for their misdemeanour. A unanimous vote against the Dingle on trial means he or she is no longer classed as a Dingle, and cannot speak, associate or live with any other Dingle. 'It stands for nothing. It's whoever is the dominating one of the day,' Lisa Riley muses. 'It works – we don't want to get in trouble with the law, so we'll sort it out ourselves. There are always loopholes, there are rules, but they waver.'

Some of the most infamous Dingle Courts across the years have involved:

1997 Marlon was found guilty of inadvertently getting Sam beaten up. He was banished, and a hate campaign was waged against him by Butch for over a year.

2003 Shadrach had let the bath overflow and damaged the Dingle home before fleeing. Returning, he was tried and banished from the family.

2003 Marlon again faced Dingle Court, this time for stealing from the sacred Dingle Pot (the pig-shaped money pot). Once again cast out of the family, he was unceremoniously thrown out into the mud.

2014 Zak exiled Charity from the family after she framed Sam's fiancée, Rachel, for the Home Farm fire.

2015 Head of the family Zak was voted out, with Cain leading proceedings, after his affair with Joanie.

2019 Mandy and Vinny faced the wrath of the Court for stealing Lydia's money.

2021 Cain orchestrated a Dingle Court and tried to nobble the voting to ensure Faith was banished, but the vote went in Faith's favour, allowing her to stay.

The Pollards & Metcalfes

1986–Present

'I've never been a family man. Always been into the next deal, and some of the deals I've made I've not exactly been proud of, and suddenly I'm given a second chance. An opportunity to put things right – it's a new beginning.'
Eric Pollard

When Eric Pollard (Chris Chittell) first arrived in Beckindale in 1986, he was a lone wolf. His marriage to Elizabeth Feldmann (Kate Dove) in 1992 was one of convenience for Eric, but estranged first wife Eileen (Arbel Jones) showed up and declared Eric a bigamist. Elizabeth was killed the following year in the plane crash fallout, leaving Eric to remarry twice in the succeeding years: to Dee de la Cruz (Claudia Malkovich) in 1997, then Gloria Weaver (Janice McKenzie) in 2002.

It would be 2006 before any of Eric's offspring emerged, when long-lost son David Metcalfe (Matthew Wolfenden) arrived. (Although in 2018, Eric would open up to Chas Dingle about a stillborn child,

Edward, that he and Eileen had had in 1978.) Despite their rocky start, David and Eric became a strong father-son unit. Eric married Val Lambert (Charlie Hardwick) in 2008, and David, having nearly married Leyla Harding (Roxy Shahidi), settled with her sister, Alicia (Natalie Anderson). Forever proposing, David also fathered a child, Amba (Ava Jayasinghe) in 2014 with previous fiancée, Priya Sharma.

After Val's death in 2015, David left Alicia to support his bereaved father, but his stepson Jacob Gallagher (Joe-Warren Plant) remained with him. 'I'm so pleased to be part of that group. Although David isn't Jacob's biological dad, he's kind of adopted him,' says Joe-Warren. 'I think they really have a good connection.'

Following his cancer treatment, David married wife number two, Tracy Shankley (Amy Walsh), in 2016, but after that marriage fell apart, he took up with Maya Stepney, who would leave their baby, Theo (Beau-Ronnie Newton), for David to raise. Currently, the three generations of the family – Eric, David and Jacob, with support from Leyla and Victoria – help to raise Theo and run the village shop. 'I enjoy writing Pollard's relationship with Jacob, having old and young relationships works and the young audience members love that,' writer Bill Lyons explains. 'There's always that idea that you can go to your grandparents with things, so I like those relationships that cross the age divide.'

Eric & Val Pollard

1986–Present & 2004-15 / Played by Chris Chittell
& Charlie Hardwick

'Valerie made me more of a person than I ever thought
I could be. She made me feel alive. Without her I am lost
in the dark again.'

Eric Pollard

Even though he's more the wise old family man these days, everyone in the Dales knows Eric Pollard's reputation as a devious, ruthless, Scrooge-like conman. 'Pollard' as he's universally, but not affectionately, known, began as a market manager and auctioneer at Hotten Market, before opening his own antiques emporium. Pollard's money driven power trip, even dabbling as mayor for a time, is almost always quashed, however. 'I loved him as a baddie, as a rotten individual. I would crease myself at some of the antics he got up to,' Chris Chittell laughs. 'The great thing about the character then was that he never got away with it and that's possibly the reason why he's been allowed to continue.'

There's not much Pollard hasn't tried over the years – from blackmail to bribery. 'I keep on being reminded by our public of some of the stuff he had the cheek to do,' Chris muses. 'There was a great moment when he had a feud with the Tates and Frank cubed Pollard's car at a breakers' yard and deposited it outside his house, and I just thought that was so ironically funny.'

Pollard's love life has been as chequered as his business dealings; first marrying Elizabeth Feldmann, before being revealed as a bigamist and then cashing in on her life insurance after her death in the plane crash – ironically, an accident that saved her from being murdered by Pollard himself. After unsuccessful marriages to Dee and Gloria, Pollard finally found the

perfect match: Valerie. No-nonsense Val was like a sledgehammer, outspoken and larger than life, 'I think possibly she was the love of his life. She pressed all his buttons. She was that vivacious and that disgraceful and she just blew Pollard away,' Chris explains. 'Charlie was great to work with, a great, gutsy actor to bounce off, as it were.' Val and Eric's pairing proved a fan favourite, as well as giving comedy gold to the writing team. 'Val and Eric were very funny people, they would always build up frustration,' Karin Young recalls. 'I loved writing for her. We have a similar voice and most people think we're sisters, and twins, which is weird!'

Following Val's premature death at the hands of a shattered mirror maze, Pollard was left alone once more, but he remains the longest-serving actor and character in the show's history. 'I'm privileged to still be part of a great body of people that care a lot about their profession,' Chris explains. 'It takes more than just a couple of people to make something so brilliant.'

David Metcalfe

2006–Present / Played by Matthew Wolfenden

'It's always the same: you get involved with women, it's always a mess. It's like you're scared to commit, someone comes along who's genuine and nice and you get cold feet and leg it.'
Jacob Gallagher

When attractive David Metcalfe first arrived in the village, turning the heads of its female residents, he was a man on a mission – to find the father he'd never known. That father was none other than Eric Pollard, and while the pair enjoy a tight, supportive and loving relationship 15 years later, initially things were fraught. Pollard had dumped David's mother before he was born, conning her out of her money, and now that she was dead, David wanted answers. Pollard was typically brusque and dismissive, earning a punch to the face. 'It was very exciting bringing David in,' Chris Chittell remembers. 'Pollard can never have realized how fortunate he was, and is, by having such a wonderfully flaky son, because he is flaky!'

Despite the shaky start, the father-son bond grew between Pollard and David, which was then mirrored when David took on his own surrogate son in the shape of Jacob Gallagher. 'They just get on so well. David's really taken him under his wing,' Joe-Warren Plant muses. This multi-generational bond was key to David facing one of his biggest challenges in 2016, when he was faced with testicular cancer, which he initially kept quiet from Jacob. Ultimately, though, they faced it together, with Jacob even choosing to shave his head alongside David when he started to lose his hair.

A chip off the old block, David has proved he's as enterprising as his father, albeit without

the deviousness and getting people's backs up. David's been a local councillor and manned a lucrative cleaning company, but his biggest business achievement is his namesake, David's Shop. A familiar sight in the village, David has run the shop since 2012, which is famed, on- and off-screen, for its distinctive 'David's Shop' branded reusable bags.

David has also followed his father's lead, possibly even exceeded him, when it comes to relationships. David's track record is lengthy to say the least, boasting relationships, flings, marriages and offspring with Delilah Dingle, Katie Sugden, Jasmine Thomas, Nicola Blackstock, Sharon Lambert, Leyla Harding, Priya Sharma, Alicia Gallagher, Tracy Shankley, Maya Stepney, Meena Jutla and Victoria Sugden since arriving in the village. 'Pollard's five-times married, so he's following in his father's footsteps,' Chris Chittell laughs. 'Every other day, David falls in love with someone else and is taken by surprise!'

Jacob Gallagher

2010–Present / Played by Joe-Warren Plant

'You're a decent man Jacob. You're a good person, kind and clever.'

Liam Cavanagh

Actor Joe-Warren Plant was eight years old when he first started in the part of Jacob Gallagher and he can't remember what his life was like before *Emmerdale*. As he has grown up on-screen, the audience has also seen Jacob develop from a sweet kid to a troubled teen, to a promising young man. 'I've been in it way more than half of my life,' Joe-Warren muses. 'When I first started out, Jacob was very much like myself: a very athletic boy, always very outgoing. As he's got older, I don't really think he's changed that much.' Originally brought in as the son of Alicia, the pair had moved to Emmerdale to join his mother's sister, Leyla, after Alicia's marriage had collapsed. However, it was only a matter of time before the secret of Jacob's true parentage would emerge – he was in fact the son of Leyla, who he'd always believed to be his aunt.

Young Jacob's tangled family tree continued to morph and, after Alicia's marriage to David Metcalfe collapsed, Jacob remained with David. Jacob has come to regard him as his 'dad', the two growing particularly close through David's cancer treatment. David provided stability as Jacob navigated adolescence, which, in typical soap style, has been littered with trauma. 'A lot has happened in his life, but at heart he's a very generous, and caring boy, because of all that's happened,' Joe-Warren explains. 'He's always been light-hearted; he does have his mood swings, quite frequently, but what kid doesn't really?!'

Jacob's biggest ordeal has been at the hands of teacher Maya Stepney, who groomed him into a sexual relationship when he was underage. Having slowly taken the journey to come to terms with that, with support from his family, Jacob found an attraction with fellow teen, Leanna Cavanagh, only to have that snatched away from him when she was killed. 'Losing Leanna, he's never really had a death with the family, so that's a new element he's experienced. It sounds bad, but it'll do him good,' Joe-Warren says. 'He's had some issues to deal with, but he'll start to come out of his shell even more.'

As one of Emmerdale's younger residents, Jacob has the potential to help forge *Emmerdale*'s future. 'I think he could be a doctor. He's a really intelligent boy and he's got all the capabilities to do that, if he can manage to apply himself,' Joe-Warren hopes.

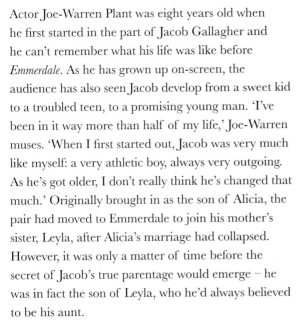

FEATURE
LEGENDS OF EMMERDALE

Every community needs its older folk, who, with colourful histories and backstories, make a great mix of characters in their own right, and the legendary older generation have given Emmerdale plenty to talk about over the years.

RODNEY BLACKSTOCK
(Patrick Mower)
Charming and flamboyant, Rodney first appeared in 2000 as the ex-husband of Diane, and father of Bernice. Rodney soon proved he had more than his share of skeletons in the closet, with the revelations that he'd fathered two more children: Nicola, with his second wife, and Paul with Diane's own sister, Val. A shameless ladies' man, age has no bounds for active Rodney. When he was a millionaire antiques dealer and vineyard owner, he lapped up the attentions of much younger Kelly Windsor, and most recently his fellow 'spirit animal', Misty Allbright. He enjoys having his daughters and grandkids close by, but mischievous Rodney shows no sign of slowing down in his golden years.

PEARL LADDERBANKS
(Meg Johnson)
For years, loud and brash vets' receptionist Pearl Ladderbanks made a formidable trio with fellow pensioners Edna Birch and Betty Eagleton. A shameless flirt, Pearl's attraction to Len Reynolds proved that happiness could be found at any age, however, fate dealt a cruel hand when Len died suddenly, leaving Pearl heartbroken. Sociable Pearl always enjoys the company of younger folk, first taking in lodger Leyla Harding, before moving into Smithy Cottage with Paddy and Rhona, then Woodbine with Edna and Harriet.

SANDY THOMAS
(Freddie Jones)
Larger than life, the weathered old sea dog Sandy Thomas couldn't have been more unlike his staid and stable vicar son, Ashley. A drinker and gambler, with many tales of his past Navy days, Sandy would often clash with Ashley over his behaviour. Ashley began taking his stresses out on his father and hit him. Off-screen, though, John Middleton was in nothing but awe of actor Freddie Jones. 'When I was told he was coming into the show, my jaw hit the desk, I'd admired him for years. He was one of the greatest character actors this country's ever produced and he became my friend.' Sandy emigrated to Australia in 2018, where he died two years later, following the passing of Freddie Jones, aged 91.

DOUGLAS POTTS
(Duncan Preston)
Laurel's father Doug was the epitome of reliability – especially when Laurel needed his strength to help her through the most traumatic events. Having first arrived as the husband of Hilary, their marriage collapsed and Doug hit a midlife crisis. Buying himself a sports car, and sleeping with a friend of Val Pollard's, Doug's uncharacteristic impulsiveness left him with an STI. Embarking on a long-term partnership with Diane Sugden, things fizzled out after a few years. Maintaining a close bond with younger members of the village, including Leyla, Gerry Roberts, Liv Flaherty and Doug's own grandson, Arthur, Doug was much missed when he made the decision to emigrate to Australia in 2020.

The Kings

2004–Present

'It doesn't have to be this way – I'm not your enemy, I'm your brother, the only one you've got left.'
'That's all very touching Jimmy, but I just don't care.'
Jimmy & Carl King

When the King family arrived, the business-focused males rode roughshod over whoever stood in their way. Self-made man Tom King (Ken Farrington) operated a haulage, security and waste-disposal company, King & Sons, and was joined by sons Jimmy (Nick Miles), Matthew (Matt Healy), Carl (Tom Lister) and Max (Charlie Kemp). 'We weren't told much about it, there was a little bit of a backstory,' Nick Miles recalls. 'Tom Lister had already been there for a month or so, he knew everybody. It's always hard to come in as the Home Farm family. Initially, people look at you like you're trampling on the grass kind of thing!'

Max, the black sheep, had shunned business and become a vet, but his stay in the village was short when he died in the crossfire between Robert and Andy Sugden's feuding, in 2005. Meanwhile, Jimmy's

scheming wife, the glamorous Sadie (Patsy Kensit) also joined the family. The Kings faced being the village pariahs when, after sabotage by Sadie, their show home development exploded and collapsed, killing three people. Tom set his sights on upper-class Rosemary Sinclair (Linda Thorson), but their marriage was brief as Tom was murdered on their wedding night. In the wake of his death, illegitimate daughter Scarlett Nicholls (Kelsey-Beth Crossley) came out of the woodwork and moved to the village with her mother, Carrie, to get to know her brothers.

By the close of 2008, Matthew had died in an accident, and the family business had gone bust. Things looked up for Jimmy, though, when he married Nicola and they had Angelica, with two more children, Elliot and Carl, popping up years later. Meanwhile, Carl's dalliance with Chas finally proved the death of him when murderous love rival Cameron Murray struck. Carl's children, Anya and Thomas, turned up for the funeral, with Thomas sticking around to terrorize Chas, who he blamed for his father's death. Together with his wife and children, Jimmy is now the last King standing, but Nick Miles isn't revelling in his survival. 'It's awful at first, because I've lost all my mates!' Nick muses. 'I think it was because Jimmy had developed into something that could be used in lots of different ways and I think that's what saved him – the comedy side, the multi-faceted character.'

Jimmy & Nicola King

2004–Present & 2001–Present / Played by Nick Miles
& Nicola Wheeler

'If I plant you in the back garden for a few months, do you think I'll get something resembling happiness?'
Nicola King

The coupling of Jimmy and Nicola is worlds apart from the characters that first appeared on-screen some 20 years ago. First established as the long-lost sister of Bernice, Nicola could easily have become a one-storyline wonder. 'Once we'd played the Nicola/ Bernice/Carlos storyline, I suggested about turning her bad,' Nicola Wheeler reveals. 'It's fun, sometimes I literally go "I can't say that!" but I will because it's hilarious. Some of her comments are just horrendous. When I'm playing her, I'm vile, because I'm leaving it for the audience to judge.'

The same can be said for Jimmy King, in that his character evolved from the hard-nosed businessman who first appeared under his father's thumb. 'It was a deliberate thing, it didn't happen overnight. Jimmy had been bullied all his life, he needed a damaging moment and the house collapse and the death of Bob's daughter to make him realize that his heart wasn't in it,' Nick Miles recalls. 'So he was a character who wanted to repent. His main weakness is women – he's hopeless, they walk all over him.' Yet despite Jimmy's early romantic failings, his chemistry with Nicola has now become *Emmerdale*'s longest-standing marriage.

'People relate to them, having tough times, staying together, perhaps doing it for the kids and then finding another way to love each other again…

however nasty Nicola can be!' Nick muses. Following the birth of daughter Angelica, Nicola and Jimmy's family has continued to grow, with Jimmy's son by Kelly Windsor, Elliot, joining them, as well as son Carl, following a mix-up at a fertility clinic. Against all the odds, including Jimmy making a pass at Bernice and Mandy on separate occasions, and Nicola overcoming her disability, the pair have weathered the challenges thrown at them, the toughest being Jimmy's amnesia, following a fight with Kelly. 'At the time we were discussing if you didn't know your partner, would you fall in love with them again, because we all change and move on,' Nicola recalls.

Despite everything, the pair have stuck together. 'They're the classic typical marriage, they have good times and bad times. They are the team – Jimmy is a little bit bullied by Nicola but he kind of likes it, he likes the woman taking control, but occasionally he takes those trousers and puts them on and puts his foot down and Nicola does listen,' Nicola says. 'And no one wants to know what goes on behind their bedroom door but I think they're slightly kinky and that's what keeps them together!'

Carl King

2004-12 / Played by Tom Lister

'I'm charmed. Bad things happen to people around me and I walk away untouched and get away with it. And I'll tell you why that is, as well, shall I? Because I'm indestructible!'
Carl King

Possessive, underhand and devious, but charming with it, arch manipulator Carl King could get away with murder...literally. One of the younger King brothers, ladies' man Carl wasted no time in getting acquainted with the females in the village, despite already having an estranged wife and two young children, Thomas and Anya, who he seemed to care as much about as the string of women he'd use and abuse. First there was Louise Appleton, then Chloe Atkinson – who lied that she was pregnant in a bid to try to keep him – before he moved on to Delilah Dingle and DCI Grace Barraclough, who was investigating his father's murder.

Carl seemingly settled down in 2010 when he married Lexi Nicholls (Sally Oliver), despite having lost his virginity decades before to her mother, Carrie. Lexi fell pregnant, but suffered an ectopic pregnancy, leaving her desperate for a child. Lexi had a breakdown, even kidnapping Jimmy and Nicola's newborn baby girl and taking her up to the hospital roof. In frustration, Carl broke up with Lexi, devastating her by revealing that he had never really loved her. Throughout all his dalliances, there had only been one woman for Carl: Chas Dingle. Despite being his biggest weakness, his one true love, he cheated on her twice, first with Chloe, then with minx Eve Jenson. For the latter, Chas enacted the perfect revenge: faking a pregnancy to get Carl down

the aisle, only to humiliate him and Eve as she jilted him at the altar, pocketing the £30,000 he'd paid out for the wedding. Carl's infatuation with Chas would ultimately be the death of him: having blackmailed Chas over her affair with Cameron Murray, she strung him along until he attempted to rape her, and she attacked him with a brick, with Cameron later finishing the job.

Ending up murdered, Carl was hardly the wronged victim; not only had he covered up the accidental death of Paul Marsden in 2004, to exonerate himself from blame, but Carl had murdered his own father. 'He did kill Tom King and once that decision had been made he pretty much became a psychopath,' Nick Miles explains. 'That was his character, after that murder, he became able to kill people without emotion.' Despite Carl's on-screen villainous persona, though, actor Tom Lister is nothing but praised by his co-star. 'He's an amazing guy, incredibly generous and friendly,' Nick adds.

FEATURE
THE KING BUSINESS

Self-made millionaire businessman Tom King arrived in Emmerdale in 2004 with his long-established family firm, King & Sons, which he ran together with sons Jimmy, Matthew and Carl. 'Jimmy was pulled out of school at the age of 16 by his dad, to help run the business, but had never reaped the rewards like his brothers had,' Nick Miles reveals. 'Jimmy was the grafter who helped build the thing, but he was treated like the thicko, unsophisticated older brother.'

Undertaking plant hire, security, waste management and disposal, King & Sons added the Home Farm Estate to their portfolio in 2005. They branched into property development in 2006, with their ill-fated Kings River Development, but that did not proceed beyond the collapsed show home. When Tom died in 2006, the business went to his sons, and a small share to illegitimate secret daughter, Scarlett. The Kings' incompetence, and in-fighting, meant they failed to fill their father's shoes and in December 2009, the business went bust. The Kings salvaged what they could and Jimmy and Carl restarted a small haulage company – Emmerdale Haulage – with one truck.

Just before his death, Carl had fallen out with Jimmy and looked to sell his 40 per cent share to

Charity Dingle, but papers weren't signed before his death, and Jimmy received everything in Carl's will. Jimmy honoured the agreement and became equal partners with Charity in the business, by now called Home James Haulage, until she sold in 2016. Robert Sugden bought her share, later turning it over to Joe Tate in exchange for £100,000 when husband Aaron was kidnapped for ransom.

Jimmy would later regain the share, but after financial difficulties in 2021, arising from court costs and a custody battle, he sold again, to Charity – Nicola having planned it behind his back. In recent years, the Kings have also bought a small share in Café Main Street, to fulfil Nicola's ambitious nature. 'Jimmy's happy to make a living, he has no aspirations for the empire as was, that's Nicola,' Nick adds. 'She thinks of him as someone who's underperforming. Jimmy's ambition is to keep his family together and happy and put food on the table.'

The Sharmas

2009–Present

'You're a disgrace. You've brought nothing but shame on this family. Until you change your ways, I no longer have son.'
Rishi Sharma

Their arrival in the village heralded a new era for the Sharma siblings, Jai (Chris Bisson) and Nikhil (Rik Makaram), as their move coincided with setting up a new factory, Sharma & Sharma. 'There were only the two brothers, and I'd come from *Corrie*, setting up the first Asian family on the street, with Rebecca Sarker playing my sister, and who would later play Manpreet' Chris Bisson recalls, 'And I set up the first Asian family on *Emmerdale*, although it is mixed race as Georgia was Caucasian.' As one of the biggest employers in the village, the Sharmas, who were joined by sister Priya (Effie Woods/Fiona Wade), were quick to integrate themselves in Emmerdale life.

Jai had caught the attention of Charity Dingle (Emma Atkins), and their engagement precipitated the arrival of the Sharma parents, Rishi (Bhasker Patel) and Georgia (Trudie Goodwin). Following the breakdown of Rishi and Georgia's marriage, Rishi became a permanent fixture. In 2011, Jai learned he had a grown-up daughter, Mia, by his best friend Declan's wife Ella. The revelation was as much a shock to Jai as to Declan, but before he could process the news properly, Mia was killed in a car crash.

Nikhil and Gennie Walker (Sian Reese-Williams) married in 2012, shortly before daughter Molly was born. Charity and Jai's marriage wasn't to last when Jai had an affair with Rachel Breckle, conceiving Archie (Kai Assi). In 2013 Nikhil became a widower when Gennie died at the hands of killer Cameron Murray. Nikhil emigrated to Canada with Molly in the

aftermath. Priya, meanwhile battled an eating disorder and, after a relationship with David Metcalfe, gave birth to Amba (Ava Jayasinghe) in 2014.

Jai wedded Megan Macey (Gaynor Faye) in 2015, but their marriage failed just before she gave birth to baby Eliza, who was born with cerebral palsy. Priya went on to marry Rakesh Kotecha (Pasha Bocarie), but he proved a lousy husband and left Priya to go on the run after committing arson.

The Sharmas saw happier times in 2019, first when Rishi married Dr Manpreet Jutla (Rebecca Sarker) and then when Jai was reunited with Archie, following Rachel's death. Manpreet's sister Meena (Paige Sandhu) joined the Sharmas in 2020, but by the following year, Manpreet and Rishi's marriage was over, when Manpreet opted to rekindle love with old flame Charles Anderson.

Jai Sharma & Laurel Thomas

2009–Present & 2002–Present / Played by
Chris Bisson & Charlotte Bellamy

'We're two addicts in recovery, we have
got five kids, all needing our attention,
and I'm sorry if I can't bright-side this.'
Laurel Thomas

The unlikely couple of the Dales, Jai Sharma and
Laurel Thomas formed a seemingly solid partnership
since first getting together, when they were boss and
secretary of the factory, in 2019. Both have quite the
colourful past, which makes their union all the more
interesting. 'I really enjoy it when Jai gets quite dark,'
Chris Bisson explains. 'He's gone off the rails, taking
cocaine, to the point he really wasn't nice and I wasn't
sure if we could salvage him. Jai's ongoing battle is
addiction and that comes through with the Laurel
story as well, because Laurel is an alcoholic. There
is mutual support there. It's important that these
characters carry these stories with them.'

Laurel meanwhile has weathered several
traumas in her life in Emmerdale, from losing a
child to cot death, to husband Ashley's struggle
with dementia. Now mother and mother figure to
Dotty, Arthur, Gabby and Archie, what started off
as a flighty, off-the-wall character has become one
of the greatest mothers the show has ever seen.
'I think the matriarchal side has evolved, and her
maternal instincts have blossomed, been challenged
and matured,' Charlotte Bellamy believes. 'Putting
characters in situations where it compromises them
is interesting, so she's always had an interesting
journey. You put alcoholism with someone who's

"good", being a soap and the character she is, the
juxtaposition makes it interesting to play.'

With life having marked both Laurel and Jai, it
was inevitable that together as a couple they would
soon face a test of their relationship. When Laurel
discovered she was pregnant in late 2020, and
they found out that the child would have Down's
syndrome, they were forced to weigh up their
situation, and whether they could cope with another
child in their blended family. 'I knew it was going
to be controversial, and that itself was a challenge,'
Charlotte recalls. 'It was written well, and we had
Leo, so the show wasn't playing one story, we
showed two sides, and it's important to show two
sides. But that's the nature of a soap, it's supposed
to cause debate.'

Whether this pair can ever fully overcome their
odds and survive as a long-term couple, remains to
be seen, but as individuals they continue to survive
whatever life has to throw at them, 'I'd love for Laurel
to stay alive for a long time in the village,' Charlotte
hopes. 'I don't want her on any bus, or train or plane!'

FEATURE
THE SHARMA BUSINESS

When brothers Jai and Nikhil Sharma arrived in the village, it wasn't just the ladies who had their eye on the new arrivals but prospective employees, too, as the pair set up a confectionery factory in the village. 'The backstory to Jai was that he was self-made and wasn't involved in the family business,' Chris Bisson explains. 'Jai had bought the family business from Rishi, much to the upset of brother Nikhil.'

Opening their chocolate empire, the factory would provide the village with plenty of work over the ten years it was in business, with jobs for the Sharmas, Laurel, Lydia, Lisa, Nicola, Kerry, Nell, Dawn, Billy, Frank, Lizzie, Joanie, Eli, Gennie, Charity and Chas, either in the office, on the floor, cleaning or out delivering. 'When the set was first built, we had conveyer belts in the factory, and the props guys used to turn them with a handle, behind the scenes,' Chris recalls. 'We did replace them with motors, but of course, in a real sweet factory the belt would be going furiously, because they'd be having to work really

hard. But in ours it was like *The Generation Game*, it would take five minutes to get down. No wonder we never made any money! They used to pack one box every five minutes, and then it would get damaged!'

The Sharmas weathered mishaps and financial traumas, but the end was close in 2019 when Rishi took a loan from Kim Tate to pay off wife Manpreet's debts, a move that proved unlucky when the factory burned down. 'The sweet factory melted, but it had been there for nearly ten years, it was going to get burned down at some point – it was a running joke for years, you know there's going to have to be a disaster.'

Jai took control to prevent bankruptcy, and having got hold of Rishi and Priya's shares, did a deal with Kim to save the business, although Jai was shocked to discover her plans to redevelop into an outdoor pursuits centre, and HOP was born. 'That's an interesting dynamic, it is a source of frustration for Jai. Jai has spent his whole life being the boss and he doesn't like being told what to do,' Chris muses.

FEATURE

MAD, BAD & DANGEROUS TO KNOW: THE VILLAINS OF EMMERDALE

There are plenty of black sheep in the legendary *Emmerdale* families, but many more remained footloose and fancy free in a line-up of the village's most notorious residents.

AL CHAPMAN (Michael Wildman)
Two-timer who cheated on Debbie and Priya, broke up Marlon and Jessie, and tried to con Chas and Marlon out of The Woolpack, only to blow it up on Christmas Day 2021.

LORD ALEX OAKWELL (Rupam Maxwell)
Cocaine-snorting lord who killed Linda Fowler when he crashed his car while high. He escaped justice but plunged off a roof to his death after a showdown with Roy Glover.

BILLY HOPWOOD (David Crellin)
Ex-convict who treated son Andy badly. Fatally injured Vic Windsor in a botched attempt to rob the post office, then went to prison.

CAMERON MURRAY (Dominic Power)
Killed love rival Carl King and went on to kill Alex Moss and Gennie Walker in order to keep his secrets covered, before escaping prison to hold The Woolpack hostage.

DECLAN MACEY (Jason Merrells)
Took revenge on wife Charity for having an abortion by trying to kill her, only to kill nephew Robbie in the process. Now on the run.

DONNY CAIRN (Alan Convy)
Lousy father of Lachlan White, who tried to get revenge for his son by starting a fire at The Woolpack, only to stab Vanessa and kidnap her son Johnny during his escape.

EMMA BARTON (Gillian Kearney)
Emma held husband James hostage before pushing him to his death on the Hotten bypass. Emma accidentally shot dead her own son, Finn, before being pushed to her death by Moira.

GORDON LIVESY (Gerard Fletcher/Gary Mavers)
Father of Aaron, who he had sexually abused when he was a child. He was convicted of the crimes, but killed himself at the start of his prison sentence.

GRAHAM CLARK (Kevin Pallister)
Graham killed his first wife, finished off lover Rachel Hughes and even tried to take Kathy with him when he plunged to his death over a cliff.

JIM LATIMER (Myles Reitherman/ Dennis Blanch)
Stalking Sharon Crossthwaite, Jim raped and murdered her, but fresh from prison in 1991, he set his sights on a new target, Sarah Connolly, before he was mercifully apprehended.

KIRIN KOTECHA (Adam Fielding/ Rish Shah)
Kirin went on the run rather than face up to killing Tess Harris in a hit and run. He returned in 2020 to try to extort money from Charity but the police caught up with him.

LACHLAN WHITE (Tom Atkinson)
Oddball Lachlan sexually assaulted Alicia Gallagher and shot his grandad, Lawrence, before killing his own mother and grandfather in a suicide-pact car crash. Lachlan claimed two more lives to cover his tracks before kidnapping girlfriend Belle, and was later imprisoned.

LEE POSNER (Kris Mochrie)
Raped Victoria Sugden and made her life hell in the aftermath until her brother Robert fatally injured him with a shovel.

MARK MALONE (Mark Womack)
Corrupt police officer who made the lives of Will, Harriet and Dawn hell, until Dawn shot him.

MAYA STEPNEY (Louisa Clein)
Teacher Maya groomed and sexually abused 16-year-old pupil Jacob Gallagher.

MEENA JUTLA (Paige Sandhu)
Meena toyed with her victims during her murder spree, killing Leanna Cavanagh, Andrea Tate and Ben Tucker, and attempting to kill Victoria, Vinny and Manpreet.

NATHAN WYLDE (Lyndon Ogbourne)
Cunning son of Mark and Natasha Wylde whose response to his father's murder was to try to pin it on half-brother Ryan. Nathan ended up with nothing and no one.

PAUL ASHDALE (Reece Dinsdale)
Compulsive gambler Paul took his anger out on son Vinny, gravely injuring him. Paul was killed when Liv Flaherty left him for dead in the barn crash and explosion.

PIERCE HARRIS (Jonathan Wrather)
Controlled and then raped wife Rhona. Fresh from prison he murdered Graham Foster and held Vanessa and her son Johnny hostage until Rhona agreed to meet him.

SALLY SPODE (Sian Reeves)
Made a play for vicar Ashley Thomas. Tried to kill his wife Laurel, twice. Her campaign ended when Laurel dangled her over her balcony, and Sally was then sectioned.

SHANE DOYLE (Paul McEwan)
Police officer involved in dodgy dealings who tried to rape Jasmine Thomas, only to be attacked by Debbie and then murdered by Jasmine. His body was dumped in Home Farm lake.

SIMON MCMANUS (Liam Ainsworth)
Drug-dealer Simon fuelled Holly Barton's drug habit, but his downfall came when he attacked Ross Barton with acid and was eventually sent to prison.

STEPH STOKES (Lorraine Chase)
Drugged and kept dad Alan a prisoner. Helped her husband Adam cover up her brother's murder, and killed her dad's girlfriend, Shelley. Currently serving a life sentence.

TERENCE TURNER (Stephen Marchant/Nick Brimble)
Brother of Steph, who had sexually abused her as a teenager. Tried to blackmail Steph's husband, Adam, but ended up dead after Adam bludgeoned him with a fire extinguisher.

CHAPTER 4

THE STORIES

'It's always adapting and showing real-life problems, and as times change, soaps change. It's still very modern, but it's all such a classic comfort just to have on. It's got a balance of old school and then still keeping up with modern times.'

Eden Taylor-Draper (*Belle Dingle*)

In a glorious village setting filled with a varied, eclectic group of characters, the rich stories of their lives organically follow: characters arrive and leave, are born and pass away, get together or break up, fall out or make up. With a current output of six episodes a week, stories are the fuel that stoke *Emmerdale*'s ever-burning fire and continue to reflect the contemporary rural life in which they're set. Whether tragic, sensitive or issue-led, dramatic, action-packed and thriller-esque, or light, comic and entertaining, *Emmerdale*'s archive bursts with a weight of well-researched, well-written, well-performed stories that strike a chord with viewers.

1970s
ON-SCREEN

First episode of *Emmerdale Farm* airs as the Sugdens gather for Jacob's funeral.

Amos Brearly and Henry Wilks begin an 18-year partnership running The Woolpack.

Peggy Skilbeck gives birth to twins.

Peggy Skilbeck dies of a brain haemorrhage.

Joe Sugden marries Christine Sharp.

1971 —— **1972** —— **1973** —— **1974** —— **1975**

David Goddard becomes the show's producer, of the first 26 episodes.

Robert D Cardona takes over as producer.

1970s
OFF-SCREEN

Emmerdale Farm has a five-month gap in broadcast from end of May to mid-October 'David Cunliffe (Executive Producer) always saw *Emmerdale Farm* as a drama series, not a soap. It wasn't until the network put pressure on it, years later, deciding whether *Crossroads* or *Emmerdale* continued to exist,' Jean Rogers explains. 'We used to have a break, because it was a series, over the summer. So when we stopped having the break we did double standing – two directors, two sets of scripts, two wardrobe assistants, etc. And you'd have location filming for one, and studio for the other. You just had to make sure you knew everything!'

The Woolpack relocates to its present building in the village.

Matt Skilbeck's twins are killed on a level crossing.

Beckindale celebrates the Queen's Silver Jubilee.

Matt Skilbeck bravely rescues trapped potholers.

The Woolpack is robbed and Amos and Henry spend the night locked in the cellar.

Matt Skilbeck marries Dolly Acaster.

The Verney family sells up and NY Estates buys Home Farm.

1976 — 1977 — 1978 — 1979

Michael Glynn takes over as producer.

Location filming is switched from Arncliffe to Esholt.

Emmerdale Farm has a break in broadcast from mid-May to January 1977.

First year that the programme is broadcast all year round.

The First *Emmerdale* book is published – *Emmerdale Farm: The Legacy*, which is a novelization of the show's first stories.

Emmerdale Farm has a break in broadcast over July and August.

Oscar James plays show's first regular black character, Tony Moeketski.

Annie's Country Diary book is published.

Anne Gibbons takes over as producer, the first female producer for *Emmerdale Farm*.

The prodigal son returns 1972

'Take it slow. I don't want Jacob bumped about on his last ride.'
Annie Sugden

The first episode of *Emmerdale Farm* established not only the core Sugden characters at the heart, but also one of the most abiding themes of the show's success: family rivalry. Within the first episode the Sugdens mourned the loss of their patriarch, Jacob, as well as dealing with the shock return of black sheep of the family, son Jack.

'The opening episode was the funeral of Annie's husband, but Donald Baverstock, Director of Programmes for Yorkshire Television at the time, wasn't keen on the first episode,' recalls Freddie Pyne. 'Kevin Laffan, the show's creator, was told "You can't start a series with a funeral!" but Kevin's response was, "Well, that's what I've done so get on with it!"' Freddie laughs.

Jacob Sugden had been the farmer of Emmerdale since before the Second World War, and together with wife Annie he had raised three children: Jack, Joe and Peggy. Jack had left eight years previously, after several rows with his father, and had moved to London, where he'd written a bestselling novel: *Field of Tares*. Jacob was an alcoholic and increasingly neglected the farm, which was run by younger son Joe, along with shepherd Matt Skilbeck, who had married Peggy.

Annie gathered the family together to mourn Jacob, and her expectation about Jack's return was fulfilled when the prodigal son arrived after the funeral service. Frazer Hines remembers filming the first scenes. 'We filmed Jacob's funeral up in the Dales, in Arncliffe. We were parked right up in a layby up in the hills, and the crew were down in the village, ready to film this funeral cortege coming all the way down the hills. So there was the funeral car and the hearse and we were waiting to start and I told a joke, as a car came past, and the look of horror on these people's faces, as they didn't know us, the show hadn't started, so all they could see was a funeral car with everyone roaring their heads off. So we decided that whenever a car went past, we'd start laughing, roaring our heads off in this funeral car, and everyone being disgusted, it was so funny.'

Murder rocks Beckindale 1973

'For the first time in my life, I looked down Beckindale High Street and felt there might be something ugly there.'
Joe Sugden

The sleepy village of Beckindale was deeply disturbed in early 1973 by the violent rape and murder of 18-year-old Sharon Crossthwaite. Unemployed loner Jim Latimer had been made redundant from a factory in Hotten and harboured a growing obsession with teenager Sharon, the daughter of Annie Sugden's cousin, Beryl. On the day of the Beckindale Sheep Dog Trials, Jim lured Sharon to the disused abbey on the edge of the village, where he made her increasingly uncomfortable as he tried to make a pass at her. Watching the altercation was local drifter Trash, who threw rocks at Jim to distract him, allowing terrified Sharon to run off and hide. Sharon waited until darkness fell, but Jim tracked her down, raping her and strangling her to death.

Only 30 episodes into the series, the crime set the precedent for the decades of shocking twists and turns that would follow. 'I recently saw the Sharon Crossthwaite episodes as someone sent me a clip,' explains Frazer Hines. 'I'm watching Jim Latimer going "Hello, where are you?" and she's hiding, and I'm thinking I'm watching a feature film. Those scenes are so tense and creepy, with Louise Jameson

hiding, they could have been taken straight from a horror film.'

Sharon was reported missing, her body undiscovered for some time, and Annie rallied support for her cousin, Beryl. Trash found Sharon's watch and showed Jack, who in turn gave it to Annie, who instantly recognized it as Sharon's. Pursued by the police as the main suspect in Sharon's death, Trash was terrified and tried to escape the Mill, falling to his death.

Jim, meanwhile, returned to stalk Penny Golightly, Trash's long-lost daughter. Alone with her at the Mill, Jim made a move on her and tried to strangle her, but was apprehended by Jack. Jim was arrested and convicted of Sharon's rape and murder, and sentenced to life imprisonment.

TIMELINE

JACK'S OLD FLAME
1972

Jack's return to Beckindale stirred up old feelings when he was reunited with Pat Merrick, who he'd left years previously when he fled to London for a new life. Pat had never stopped loving Jack, despite having married Tom Merrick, with whom she had two children (although son Jackie would later be revealed to be Jack's son). Tom was a lousy husband, a drunk, openly violent towards Pat and jealous of Jack's return to the village. Tom probed about Jack and Pat's relationship as they reminisced over old times, and despite Pat's protestations that she had no feelings for him, Tom knew she still held a torch for Jack. Pat pressured Jack to sack Tom, who had now realized Jackie was Jack's son, and the Merricks packed up for a new start away from the village.

TRASH THE TRAMP
1973

Jack initially shunned farm life, instead moving to a derelict millhouse on the edge of Emmerdale land, planning to renovate it. He found a like-minded creative soul in the shape of Ian McIntyre, known as 'Trash' since abandoning his life as a librarian and leaving his wife and daughter. Jack and Trash indulged in a bohemian lifestyle, but when Trash was embroiled in the disappearance and death of Sharon Crossthwaite, Jack's second cousin, he panicked. Having implicated himself by having Sharon's watch, Trash protested his innocence to Jack, and Reverend Ruskin, before hiding in the Mill to evade police suspicion. Fearful of what would happen, Trash jumped from a window, killing himself. Jack was profoundly affected by Trash's passing, and paid for his funeral.

THE SUGDENS VS THE GIMBELS
1975

The Sugdens had always got on well with their immediate neighbours at Holly Farm, the Gimbels, but when tyrannical Jim Gimbel was overusing fertilizer and it affected Emmerdale's land, a feud developed. Annie had always shared lifts to Hotten with Jim's wife Freda, but following the growing feud, the arrangement stopped and Annie was spurred on to learn to drive and buy her own car. Hostilities reached a high when Joe began a relationship with Jim and Freda's married daughter, Kathy, and they set up home together. Jim became increasingly bitter and when some sheep from Emmerdale wandered onto his land through a break in the drystone wall, Jim refused to return them until he was paid compensation. Battlelines were drawn between Emmerdale Farm and Holly Farm.

Peggy and Matt's joy is short-lived

1973

'It's Peggy. I don't know what to do. She's just lying on the floor. I can't wake her.'
Matt Skilbeck

Things were on the up for the Skilbecks: following her father Jacob's death, Peggy had discovered she was pregnant, with twins. Peggy and husband Matt were thrilled, and after Peggy received a share in Emmerdale Farm following the reshuffle of business shares, she hoped to sell hers to fund a new and more exciting city life. But stick-in-the-mud Matt wanted to continue to work the land, so the pair compromised and moved to Hawthorn Cottage, a farmhouse on the edge of Emmerdale's land, recently acquired by Emmerdale Farm Ltd, and began renovating it.

Peggy gave birth to a boy and girl, Sam and Sally, in April 1973, just before the lambing season, making Annie a grandmother for the first time. Peggy's grandfather, Sam Pearson, was particularly touched that the baby boy was named after him.

Only three months later, tragedy would strike the Skilbecks and Sugdens, when Peggy, complaining of a headache, went to bed, only for Matt to find her dead a few hours later. Peggy had died of a brain haemorrhage, aged only 24, leaving Matt a widowed father of two babies.

The Sugdens relied heavily on each other, and friends such as Amos, Henry and Reverend Ruskin, in the aftermath, no one able to fathom how a young healthy life could have been lost. Peggy was buried with her father and Matt returned to live at Emmerdale Farm with his children.

Matt tried to move on, later beginning a relationship with barmaid-turned-shopkeeper, Alison Gibbons, but after a year together, they ended the relationship.

Joe's brief encounter 1974

'Why are they all sat on one side?'
'That's the bride's side – there's none
of hers here.'
Matt Skilbeck & Joe Sugden

In charge at Emmerdale Farm, Joe pushed for modernization, wanting the herd to have accredited status. When the Milk Marketing Board sent official Christine Sharp to test the cows, Joe quickly fell for her. After a whirlwind romance, the couple made plans to marry, and Christine quit her job and moved into the farmhouse. The fly in the ointment was Christine's dad, Robert, a wealthy landowner with a dairy empire, who disliked Joe, thinking he was not good enough for his daughter. When Robert refused to come to the wedding, Joe and Christine married anyway, within a year of meeting, with Henry Wilks stepping in to give Christine away. Returning from a honeymoon in London, the newlyweds set up home at Matt and Peggy's old house, Hawthorn Cottage. Frazer explains the rather rushed and sudden union of Christine and Joe, 'I was supposed to marry Carol Benfield, a friend of Janie Harker (Pat Sugden's sister), but Ann Holloway (Carol) went to London for the weekend with straight blonde hair and came back with a perm. The producer at the time, Robert D Cardona, went up the wall, so they found a wig, but it didn't work. But they had the scripts for this marriage, so they grabbed Angela Cheyne (Christine), who'd been in a couple of episodes.'

Frazer admits his shock at the switch, 'Bob Cardona said I was going to marry Christine, but I said "Well, I hardly know her", but they decided to rewrite the scripts and make it a short marriage anyway, so I felt that made a lot more sense.' Sure enough, cracks began to form in the marriage: Joe struggled to provide the same level of material wealth that Christine's father had and he was appalled when she refurnished their new home using her father's money. After tensions and disagreements, Christine left Joe, after only five weeks of marriage, fleeing Beckindale in her sports car.

Jackie's world is rocked 1982

'We ought to get on better, Jackie
– I am your father.'
Jack Sugden

When Jack Sugden had walked out on Emmerdale Farm and Beckindale in 1964, he'd left behind girlfriend Pat Harker (originally called Ruth), who found herself pregnant. Desperate to provide herself and her baby with stability, she married Tom Merrick, and despite naming the baby John Jacob (the same name as Jack!), she kept his paternity a secret from everyone. Seventeen years later, having returned to Beckindale and having had flings with Marian Wilks and Laura Verney, Jack found Pat always on his periphery, as she endured a loveless marriage with her abusive husband. When Pat blurted out the truth about teenage son Jackie's paternity during a row with Jack at the end of 1981, it was only a matter of time before Jackie himself would find out from his newly returned dad.

Jackie, played by Ian Sharrock, had joined *Emmerdale Farm* in 1980. 'I knew all about Jackie's real father when I did that first interview, so it was no shock for me!' laughs Ian. Struggling to process the news, Jackie couldn't accept Jack, and his assumed father, Tom, shunned him. Seth Armstrong took wayward Jackie under his wing, teaching him how

to be a gamekeeper, but Jackie resorted to drinking, fighting and torching the NY Estates caravan, which left him with a criminal record. 'Jackie went a bit weird, because he had been raised by Tom Merrick, he always wanted the approval of his dad, like most teenage boys, but Tom wasn't a very good dad, he was rough, unreliable and free with his hands, not father material really,' Ian explains. 'He didn't have to try at all with Jack. But Jackie was annoyed at this guy muscling in and getting together with his mum.' Initially against Pat's planned marriage with Jack, it would take Jackie years to gradually accept Jack as his father.

Meanwhile, Ian's position as the young heartthrob of *Emmerdale Farm* was firmly determined during the 1980s. '*The Yorkshire Post* called Jackie "The James Dean of the Dales", and I thought, "yeah, I'll have that!"' Ian laughs. 'It was enormous fun. It was a challenge – I was back in school uniform aged 20. Suddenly at 20 I wasn't allowed in pubs, because they all thought I was 16!'

TIMELINE

JACK FINALLY SETTLES DOWN
1982

Annie Sugden never thought she'd see the day her footloose eldest son would marry, but as the dust settled surrounding the revelation that Jack had fathered a son, Jackie, he and Jackie's mother, Pat, finally decided to tie the knot. Pat had left her abusive husband Tom and finally divorced him, however, Reverend Donald Hinton refused to marry them as Pat was a divorcee. Undeterred, the pair married in Hotten Register Office instead, surrounded by family.

SANDIE'S PREGNANCY
1983

Sixteen-year-old Sandie Merrick found herself pregnant and confided in her shocked brother, Jackie, that the father was Andy Longthorn, Jackie's former schoolmate and the son of a local farmer. Protective Jackie reacted badly and beat Andy up, while the Sugdens decided Andy should surrender his place at university and do the right thing: marry Sandie and settle down to raise the child. Overwhelmed, Sandie went to Aberdeen, where her father Tom was working on oil rigs, and gave birth to a baby girl away from gossips and family pressures. Sandie returned to the village having given up baby Louise for adoption.

TURNER MEETS HIS MATCH
1984

Alan Turner had quickly gained a reputation for himself as the man at the helm of Home Farm, and his assistants struggled to control his amorous urges and debauchery. Threatened with dismissal, Alan wiped the slate clean, and under the careful control of new secretary Caroline Bates, he turned over a new leaf. Alan's first attempt at reconciling his behaviour was to try to make up with his estranged wife, Jill, and his children. Unsuccessful, Alan later turned his attentions to developing a more honourable and meaningful relationship with Caroline.

Emmerdale loses its 'Grandad' 1984

'We all have duties, and one of those is to stick by your flesh and blood.'

Sam Pearson

For over ten years, Sam Pearson was the lovable old rogue of *Emmerdale Farm*. Annie's father, affectionately known as 'Grandad', Sam was the standard bearer for all the old village customs and traditions. A retired farm manager, Sam could turn his hand to most things, making a recorder out of an old table leg and a rabbit hutch for his infant great-grandchildren's animals. Resistant to change, Sam could be perceived as a grump: he heavily objected to favourite grandson Joe 'living in sin' with Kathy Gimbel, and even the installation of a telephone in the Emmerdale farmhouse was met with hostility!

Above all else, Sam was a family man, so it was a dark, sad day for the Sugdens when, in November 1984, the morning after he'd won first prize for his pumpkin in Beckindale's annual show, Annie found Sam had died in his sleep. The family united, with Joe returning from working abroad to pay his respects, and Sam was buried in the Beckindale cemetery.

As the Sugdens mourned the loss of Sam, so did the cast that actor Toke Townley had worked with, following Toke's passing in September 1984, aged 71. 'Jean (Dolly) rang me to say, "have you heard about Toke?" and I said "no", and she said "well, he's died of a heart attack in the middle of Leeds",' Freddie Pyne remembers. 'I burst into tears, I really loved him, he was a very English eccentric.'

'Toke was a film actor, in old black-and-white films,' explains Frazer Hines. 'He was a great flautist, so again, the writers brought that in, Grandad playing the flute. He was a great one for not knowing his lines completely and going around the hills and coming back again. One day he jumped on the table in the rehearsal room and fell off and broke his leg! He was a fun person to be with.'

Freddie recalls, 'Toke once said to me, "my accountant told me to do a couple more years and then I'll have enough for a good pension"…But of course that never happened for him.'

TIMELINE

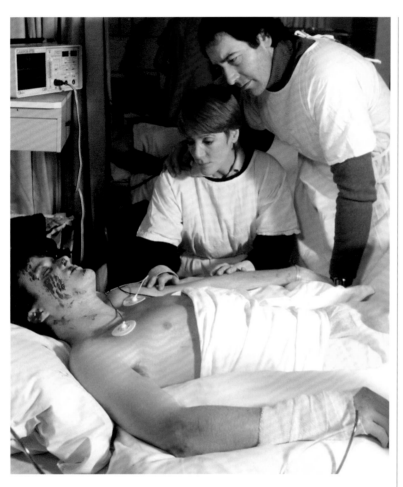

DOLLY REUNITES WITH HER BOY
1986

Dolly fell pregnant again in 1985, but at the time she was caught up in the Sugdens' feud with local quarry owner, Harry Mowlam. When he made improper advances to Dolly, the stress of the incident became a factor in her miscarriage, leaving her devastated at another chance of motherhood dashed. Dolly was shocked when her long-lost son, Graham Lodsworth, who she'd given up for adoption 20 years previously, tracked her down, having deserted his job in the army to find his birth mother. Absent without leave, Graham went to ground, living rough in the woods, even torching his own car to avoid detection. Dolly was upset when Graham's sergeant major found him and returned him to the army barracks.

JACKIE'S NEAR-DEATH EXPERIENCE
1985

While at a barn party, Jackie and his girlfriend Alison broke up, leaving Jackie to slink off early. Riding home on his motorbike, the lights failed, and on a corner of a dark country lane, Jackie and his bike were no match for Alan Turner and his Range Rover. Suffering broken bones and concussion, Jackie was seriously injured. His near-death experience helped mellow hostilities between Jackie and Jack, and Jackie began to call Jack 'Dad' for the first time. Jackie spent five months in hospital, where he met and fell in love with nurse Sita Sharma. The pair became engaged, but Sita ultimately ended things after she felt pressured by Jackie.

Pat Sugden's tragic end 1986

'Jack, will you stop it, what you trying to do? Going through all that stuff isn't going to bring her back. We can all remember the things we said, or didn't say, the things we did or didn't do, it's not going to bring her back!'
Sandie Merrick

In the aftermath of Jack Sugden's affair with Karen Moore, Jack had chosen to commit to wife Pat and they found themselves expecting a baby. Robert Jacob Sugden was born in April 1986, and the following month he was christened, with Dolly, Joe and Amos as godparents.

Yet a mere four months after the joyous event for the Sugdens, fate would take another tragic turn, much as it had done years previously when Jack's sister died soon after the birth of her twins. Pat was driving her sister, Janie, back to the train station after her visit to Emmerdale Farm. On her way back, Pat overtook a milk lorry and, speeding, came across a sheep blocking the road. Pat swerved and flew off the hillside at speed, her little Ford Fiesta rolling violently down the hill, killing her.

Widowed Jack, with a baby son and an older family with son Jackie and stepdaughter Sandie, faced life after losing Pat in a sudden, freak accident, 'The writers always came up with things, brave things, brave and sensitive stories,' Malandra Burrows muses. 'As an actor, you know they've been researched and touch a lot of people who are going through it

themselves.' In the aftermath, Sandie broke down, while Jackie remained strong, whereas Jack, with resounding guilt as he was the one that was supposed to have made that journey, fell into deep depression. Jack could not face looking at baby Robert, and kept dreaming about the funeral, before finally disappearing from the farm. Jack turned up at his brother Joe's house and he helped him to process his feelings over Pat's death. With further support from Annie, Jack began to reunite with his baby son as he faced raising him as a single father.

TIMELINE

SANDIE'S AFFAIR
1986

Sandie Merrick began a relationship with Phil Pearce, a married builder, causing consternation from step-grandmother Annie Sugden, who made her leave Emmerdale Farm. Phil left his wife and he and Sandie set up together at Mill Cottage. Phil and Joe established a business together, Phoenix Developments, and their first project was renovating Mill Cottage.

MATT FALLS UNDER SUSPICION
1986

When local farmer Harry Mowlam was killed, Matt was horrified to find himself in the frame for murder after a fight between the two about Mowlam's sheep rustling had been widely witnessed – Matt had stopped the theft of sheep and the two had fought badly, as Harry had goaded him. Matt was charged with manslaughter, but he was proved innocent when Harry's associate, Derek Warner, was revealed to be the murderer. Derek had killed Harry after a row about loot from a robbery, and Derek's story was backed up when the £6,000 was found in Harry's pig shelter. Derek confessed, but not before he'd held Reverend Donald Hinton hostage in the vicarage in his attempt to escape.

JOE'S READY-MADE FAMILY
1988–89

Joe became interested in recently divorced Kate Hughes, and after a series of unfortunate incidents, including Joe shooting her dog Rex, the pair got together. Kate and her teenage children, Mark and Rachel, moved into Emmerdale Farm and Joe and Kate married; Reverend Hinton relaxing the no-divorcee rule. Wayward Mark didn't initially approve and ran off to find his father, David, in Germany, but didn't get further than Hull.

POLLARD LETS PHIL TAKE THE FALL
1988

Nick Bates foiled a robbery at the post office, but, tempted by the spoils, he pocketed some of the loot himself. Entrusting the cash to his girlfriend, Nick was ripped off when she disappeared with the money, leaving him at the mercy of Eric Pollard and Phil Pearce, who learned of his part in the crime and made life difficult for him. Meanwhile, Pollard and Phil planned a robbery at Home Farm, stripping out antique fireplaces. Pollard kept Caroline Bates and Alan Turner busy with carol singing while Phil broke in, using Caroline's keys, and ripped out the fireplaces, storing them until the dust settled. Nick fingered Pollard and Phil for the crime, and while moving the fireplaces, Phil was arrested. Phil confessed to his part in the con and Pollard, with no evidence against him, let Phil take the fall.

Beckindale goes nuclear 1987

'My reason is in the families, in the farm, in the fields and the crops, and the animals, and my argument is in my son, in the children and the young people of Beckindale...Our only position is "no", our only reason is "no", and our only argument is "no"!'
Jack Sugden

The late 1980s saw Beckindale faced with wider world issues, when the villagers fought against the government's proposals to dump nuclear waste in the village. Jack Sugden, flying the flag for agriculture and the environment, led the troops to battle against the plans, while Dolly Skilbeck, as co-ordinator for the local playgroup, rallied the concerned mothers of the neighbourhood, focusing on the effects that the plans would have on the next generations.

An initial protest meeting was called, for residents to air their grievances, and young and old alike were in unison with their fears, with Archie Brooks and Jack in particular being the most vocal. Tests began on land at Pencross Fell, and the villagers, not wanting any risk from the nuclear waste, set up a protest camp, complete with a headquarters in a caravan, and placards with 'Say No to a Shallow Grave' and 'Beckindale Says No to Radioactive Waste' daubed on them.

As the contractors' convoy approached, lookouts Seth and Archie burst into a church service to mobilize their army of angry protestors. A 'broken-

down' tractor and a flock of sheep were drawn in to block the builders' routes, but the protest turned ugly and Jack was arrested. The protest was ultimately a success when the plans were scrapped, but Jack ended up imprisoned in Armley jail for contempt of court. When he was released, Jack was surprised to have gained the approval of his mother, Annie, who'd been in hospital after a knee operation, for taking a militant stand. 'I'd completely forgotten about that storyline,' Malandra Burrows laughs. 'But look how that stands even today, with pushing important environmental issues. So even back then, in the early days, we were doing that.'

Dolly's dream goes up in smoke 1987-88

'Crossgill still burnt down today, while we just stood there and watched. We had such plans for that place and now we're right back where we started; all our hard work just thrown in our faces. It's gone Matt, it's gone.'
Dolly Skilbeck

Matt Skilbeck got a rare bout of luck when he inherited the farm of reclusive neighbour, Metcalfe, who he'd helped out from time to time. Dolly was thrilled at the idea of a home of her own, and she and Matt had builder Phil Pearce renovate the farmhouse at Crossgill. Jean Rogers explains, 'It was all rather wonderful for Dolly. She was a young wife, with a baby and living under the same roof as Matt's first mother-in-law. They got on so well, but Annie would be popping in all the time and I think Dolly needed a place of her own, and Crossgill was going to be the chance for her and Matt's relationship to move on.'

Annie went to see how the house was shaping up, unaware that Phil had left rags near a naked flame. She became trapped when the house caught fire. Alerted to the fire by Sandie, Phil and Dolly rushed to rescue Annie, Phil making amends for his carelessness by leading Annie to safety, who recovered from her smoke inhalation. The house burned down, leaving Dolly devastated, although Matt was secretly relieved at not having to leave his home at Emmerdale.

'Matt and Dolly started to drift emotionally,' Jean recalls, 'Dolly was growing and needing more.' Annoyed and disappointed at Matt's failure to support her dreams, Dolly took up with tree surgeon Stephen Fuller. After they went on a secret trip together, Dolly confessed all to Annie and ended the affair. 'The tree-feller fella, as I used to call him, was giving her that kind of attention that she wasn't getting from lovely Matt,' Jean explains. 'Michael Russell wrote those six episodes with Dolly and Stephen – we called them Dolly's brief encounter, to stand on their own, from the beginning to when she lets him go.'

Dolly was later gutted to discover Stephen had died, by a falling tree. Jean recalls, 'I had a fan letter through when they killed him off, from a woman who said, "I am never going to watch *Emmerdale* again, I always do my ironing at 7 o'clock, and I've so enjoyed this storyline, and I've waited for Stephen and Dolly to go off and make mad passionate love, so I couldn't believe it when he was just killed off like that."'

In turning her back on Stephen Dolly had surrendered her dream for reality and loyalty to her family, just as Annie had done decades previously. But the days of the Skilbecks' marriage were numbered.

Viv's past comes back to haunt her

1994

'I won't get out of here alive, you know that. And I'm not letting you out of here without me.'

Reg Dawson

Viv Windsor had hoped for a new start when her family moved to Beckindale, but her quiet life came crashing down by the reappearance of ex-con, ex-husband Reg Dawson. Fresh out of prison, Reg looked to reconcile with Viv and son Scott, professing to have found God, but all the while planning an armed robbery.

Reg and two masked raiders robbed the post office, taking Viv hostage when she got in the way, pausing for a street shoot-out with shotgun-wielding Joe Sugden. As Reg and his crew fled across the Dales, Joe, Vic and the mounting police operation were stunned when the post office and shop exploded – Reg having caused a gas leak. 'The director, Graham Wetherell, told me to creep up as it blows up,' recalls Frazer Hines. 'I said can we have a rehearsal, and he said no, we're going to blow it in one take, when you hit that rock. Ian Rowley was in charge so you knew you were safe. I crept up behind the post office, turned my back, hit the rock and threw myself up in the air, and that's when it exploded.'

On the run, Reg came across Shirley Turner in her Range Rover and held her at gunpoint as he got her to drive them to Home Farm, empty as the Tates were on holiday. Surrounded by armed police, Reg and his associates held Shirley and Viv hostage – an unhinged Reg shooting one accomplice dead, and the other surrendering to police. As Shirley tried to calm Reg, she kept him sweet by dressing up in Kim's expensive clothes, and eventually slept with him. As Reg was desperate to be reunited with Viv, even if that meant in death, Shirley intervened and was killed when Reg shot her. Thinking her time was up too, Viv braced herself for death, but the police marksmen stormed the house just in time, shooting Reg dead and reuniting Viv with bereft Vic.

'I was so pleased to get such a big storyline, because I'd only just arrived,' Deena says. 'It was either sink or swim, because I was the new girl in, I hadn't done a soap before, so I had to understand the way they worked. I just embraced it and went for it. It was fantastic, it was like doing a little film.'

Seth & Betty's non-wedding 1994

'I want it known, that from now, Betty and me are officially a couple.'
Seth Armstrong

Seth Armstrong and Betty Eagleton had reunited in 1994, following the deaths of their respective spouses, having once been together before the war. They'd come close to marrying in the 1940s, before Betty went off to London to work as a tiller girl. Back together with Betty after 50 years apart, Seth threw caution to the wind and asked her to marry him. Having won the approval and consent of Betty's father, they planned a wedding, but at the last minute got cold feet. Deciding there was no point in the formality and fuss of marriage at their time of life, they opted instead to remain as they were, enjoying 'keeping up with the younger folk' in living together unmarried.

Not wanting to disappoint the whole village, who had turned out to wish them well, Seth and Betty went ahead with the party in the village hall, a 1944-themed event to celebrate what would have been 50 years of marriage had they wed when they first met. All of their friends and neighbours turned out to party with them, dressed in 1940s' costumes, with Betty as a 40s' bride and Seth in the uniform of an American colonel.

The party was fraught with some tensions, though, as Chris Tate opted to bring new lover Rachel Hughes, and announced to his father that Rachel was expecting his baby. Spurned, estranged wife Kathy fumed to see the couple out in public, but she had been dealing with her upset and anger by yearning for married doctor Bernard McAllister, who she believed was in love with her. 'Kathy having a thing for the doctor was a weird story!' Malandra Burrows laughs.

'I can forgive Kathy for the doctor thing, she just went completely off the rails. Anyone in that situation would have duveted, box of chocolates and prosecco, but *Emmerdale* style, she went for the doctor instead!'

Kim spooks Frank to death 1997

'You're a dinosaur, Frank. And you know what happened to them.'
Kim Tate

Kim had been genuinely devastated by the death of her lover, Dave, at the end of 1996 and her grief soon turned to bitterness and anger at being stuck with Frank, desperate to believe that he was not the father of her baby. Kim began to make life as difficult as possible for Frank – refusing to leave Home Farm, and reporting him to Inland Revenue, but then, after a fight, Kim just disappeared. A police investigation emerged, and her car was found at the bottom of the quarry, with a body inside. Frank and Zoe identified the decomposing corpse as Kim. Kim was given a funeral, buried, and Frank was imprisoned for her murder – only let out on bail after receiving a beating in prison.

Months later, out of the blue, Kim walked into Home Farm, stunning Frank. Kim hid his heart medication and explained how she had faked her death – she had paid a double to drive her car back to the village and dump it in the quarry. What Kim hadn't counted on was the woman becoming trapped in the car and dying, and a body being recovered. Meanwhile, Kim had been in Mauritius, biding her time until her return. Kim taunted Frank – she knew

she could just disappear again and no one would be any the wiser. The shock of seeing Kim again instigated a fifth and final heart attack for Frank. Kim casually checked if he was breathing using her compact mirror, before touching up her make-up and calmly vanishing again. Kim returned on the day of Frank's funeral to make her return public and permanent, solidifying her status at Home Farm as she inherited Frank's estate.

Claire King muses on her character's return from the dead, 'I'd actually left and then I got a call over the Christmas break, saying would I consider coming back, but I said "You're burying me on Monday!"' Writer Bill Lyons explains the behind-the-scenes considerations, 'It was convincing when she died because as far as we were concerned, she had! The executive producer then came in and said "There's been a small change. You all thought Kim's dead, but actually she's not". We had to then work from there, it wasn't planned!' Uniquely, one of the only physical traces of Kim's fake death now resides with Claire, 'I've actually got the coffin plaque in my loo,' she laughs.

TIMELINE

ANDY FINDS A FAMILY
1997–98

Andy Hopwood had really gelled with the Sugdens following his trip to their farm and his visits turned to a fostering placement when his grandmother died. But as Andy settled into farm life, his wayward father, Billy Hopwood, turned up, fresh from prison. Billy took Andy to live in a remote caravan, leaving him alone to fend for himself while he undertook several (mainly illegal) jobs. Isolated from the Sugdens, Andy was neglected, and once his dad abandoned him, he was grateful to return to Jack and Sarah. Billy returned a year later, again full of big plans and grand schemes, tapping Andy for money and food while planning an armed robbery at the post office; a move that saw Vic Windsor attacked and killed. Billy was apprehended and returned to prison after Andy turned him in.

KIM & STEVE LOSE IT ALL
1998

Kim Tate thought she'd found Mr Right with suave financial whizz Steve Marchant, but his financial risks flopped and he lost everything on their wedding day. Practically bankrupt, Kim sold off her Home Farm shares and lowered her sights as she moved into Steve's modest cottage. Looking to claw back their wealth, Kim and Steve masterminded a plot to steal Kim's racehorse, sell it and pocket the insurance money as well. Their practised plan seemed flawless, until Steve accidentally hit Kathy with the horsebox during the getaway. Kim tried to keep control, even stopping Steve from smothering the comatose Kathy. As the net closed in, Kim cunningly let Steve take the fall, even hiding the robbery loot from him in a bid to ensure her own freedom, but their futures

looked bleak when they were both charged with the robbery.

THE WOOLPACK BURNS
1998

Alan Turner thought he'd left his beloved pub in safe hands for the evening with his recently arrived granddaughter Tricia and bar manager Terry, but they hosted an after-hours lock-in for the regulars before heading upstairs. As Terry believed he'd worked his charms on attractive Tricia, their passion was thwarted by a commotion downstairs – they'd left a candle burning, which had ignited fireworks left in the bar by Tricia. The fireworks display gutted the bar, shooting out of the windows and causing minor injury to passing Eric Pollard. When Alan returned, he was as gutted as his pub and, refusing to believe Tricia could be responsible, he sacked long-term manager Terry. As The Woolpack was refurbished, Alan brought in temporary barmaid Bernice Blackstock, who would later rise the ranks to bar manager and then landlady.

Kim makes a break for freedom 1999

'Kim Marchant?'
'No, Kim Tate.'
Helicopter pilot & Kim Tate

Kim and Steve Marchant's foiled plan to recoup their wealth by stealing Kim's own racehorse, selling it and pocketing the insurance money had left Steve imprisoned for his accidental hit-and-run on Kathy, and Kim also on trial for fraud. Facing a conviction, shrewd Kim was determined not to go down, and having hidden the robbery loot in Frank's grave, planned to make a bid for freedom with baby James on the eve of the verdict. But as she went digging for treasure, Kim discovered Chris, hellbent on seeing her go to prison, had uncovered her get-out-of-jail-free card. Confronting him at Home Farm, Kim tried threatening him, playing for sympathy, even seducing him, before resorting to a spot of attempted murder to get her way.

Grabbing the £190,000, and leaving Chris to die, Kim bade farewell to the Dales, making a dramatic exit with James in a helicopter, as Chris clawed across the driveway of Home Farm, desperate to stop his wicked stepmother. Kim flew to freedom, satisfied that she'd once again had the last laugh.

Claire King recalls the day of shooting Kim's exit: 'It was great, I actually took a bag of vegetable soup with me from the caterers and pretended that I'd been sick in the helicopter when I landed!' Claire laughs. 'I got to fly around the whole village and the countryside, and I could see my house! It was a fabulous exit.'

TIMELINE

KELLY'S TRAIL OF DESTRUCTION
1998–2000

Kelly Windsor had always had a turbulent time with men: pregnant by Biff, she'd led rich Chris Tate to believe he was the father, hoping he'd pay for an abortion, only to lose the baby after a scuffle with Kim at Home Farm. Through it all, Roy Glover had always been infatuated with Kelly, only for her to keep him at arm's length. When stepbrother Scott returned from the army with a womanizing reputation, he pursued Kelly, leading to an illicit kiss at Christmas while Kelly's father lay dying after a robbery at the post office. Regret soon grew to temptation and Scott and Kelly slept together. Disgusted, Kelly tried to distract herself by throwing her energies into a relationship with Roy, leading to a quick marriage. Unable to resist, Kelly slept with Scott again and she became pregnant – unsure if the father was Roy or Scott. Kelly attempted suicide, but survived. Roy and Kelly planned a new life in Ibiza, but after discovering her on-off affair with Scott, Roy left the village alone.

BUTCH GETS HIS GIRL
1999–2000

Village misfit Butch Dingle was delighted to find his equal in shy and timid Emily Wylie, who started work at the shop. As they began a tentative courtship, aided by Betty, it quickly emerged that Emily was under the spell of her abusive tyrant of a father, farmer John Wylie. Butch defended Emily's right to freedom, resulting in a fight when John tried to keep the lovers apart. Butch and John embarked on a country lane car chase and as John crashed, Butch saved him and Emily before the Land Rover exploded. John gradually began to mellow as he spent more time with Butch and the Dingles, leaving Emily and Butch to fall deeply in love, hopeful of their happily ever after.

ZOE TURNS KILLER
1999

Mysterious Liam Hammond, a lorry driver at Tate Haulage, kidnapped his boss, Chris Tate, and held him hostage. Chris assumed it was for a ransom, but as Liam showed Chris newspaper

cuttings about the Tates from across the years, and photos of Liam's mum with Frank, Liam revealed he was Chris's half-brother. Liam held Chris prisoner for over a month and as Chris started to get Stockholm syndrome and bond with his newfound brother, Zoe began to twig Liam's obsession with Chris. Shocked to find Chris in Liam's cellar, Zoe defended herself and Chris, and shot Liam dead. Stunned at her own actions, Zoe and Chris destroyed all the evidence of their connection to Liam, but Chris, upset at Zoe having caused Liam's death, arranged his funeral and buried him next to Frank. Zoe and Chris claimed self-defence and despite the investigations of DI Spalding, seasoned in investigating the Tates' misdeeds, Zoe walked free. The incident would profoundly affect Zoe, leading to her breakdown and descent into schizophrenia.

Chris Tate's final scheme 2003-4

'I'll never forgive you for as long as I live, and I'll hate you even longer. I'll despise you for eternity. So, I propose a toast: to the death of our marriage.'
Chris Tate

Chris Tate had put up with a lot from wild-card wife Charity, in particular the revelation that Paddy and Emily's teenage foster daughter Debbie was Charity's lovechild with second cousin Cain. But the final nail in the coffin, literally for Chris, was discovering that Cain and Charity had rekindled their affair. 'I think he genuinely loved Charity,' explains Peter Amory. 'She may have been his real love and that's why he was so affected by the fact that she betrayed him.'

Chris was soon dealt another blow: he had an inoperable brain tumour and only months to live. Chris wanted the ultimate revenge on his cheating wife: to frame her for his murder. Inviting her over to discuss reconciliation, he put on the performance of a lifetime, including a distressed secret call to the police, and ensuring Charity's fingerprints were on a champagne flute filled with poison. Spewing hatred for Charity, Chris downed the toxic drink and died in a macabre scene on the floor at Home Farm, uttering his final word: whore.

Peter recalls his decision to leave the show after 14 years, 'I had nothing against the programme, I just wanted to move on. So the producers asked for time to write me out. I said, yeah, take a few weeks, but I had about five more contracts. I'd get towards the end

of one and think, it's not wrapping up!' laughs Peter. 'And then I met with the producer, Steve, and asked how Chris would go and he said, "You're going to frame Charity". We laughed a lot about that!'

Charity was arrested, tried and convicted of Chris's murder, then sentenced to life imprisonment. Having discovered she was pregnant, Charity gave birth in prison, unsure about the baby boy's paternity. When Chris was proven to be the father, Charity struck a deal with Zoe: in exchange for the baby, who Zoe named Christopher, and £10,000, Zoe would provide a statement testifying Chris had killed himself.

Charity was freed, but Debbie, discovering the deal, disowned her mother and burned the £10,000. Charity got together with Tom King and as she began to develop feelings for her baby, now called Noah, encouraged by Tom, she went for custody when the courts refused to grant it to Zoe. 'What I didn't know when I left, was that Charity was pregnant,' adds Peter. 'I'd have put money on the fact that I had one son, Joseph, and then recently I was told no I've got two, but I said look I played it, I've got one! I didn't find out about Noah until last year!'

Stormy weather hits Tricia 2003-4

'I came back, Marlon!'
Tricia Dingle

After several hiccups, Marlon and Tricia had finally married in early 2003, but after only a few months of wedded bliss, Tricia took a role in a Bollywood film and jetted off to India. Returning home to her beloved Marlon at the end of the year, she was devastated when he revealed a one-night stand with second cousin Charity. Tricia and Marlon split and while Tricia made plans to leave the village on New Year's Eve, Marlon tried everything, from a new home to a stray puppy, in a bid to win back his wife.

While the residents gathered in The Woolpack to celebrate Donna Windsor's 18th birthday, the wind and rain outside turned to a treacherous storm, soon claiming its first casualties, when Ashley Thomas and Louise Appleton crashed their car into the river, leaving them trapped and Ashley severely injured and unconscious. Meanwhile, waiting for her lift out of the village for good, Tricia paused to read Marlon's last-ditch attempt to persuade her to stay: a letter of 101 things he loved about her. Losing pages of the letter in the gales, Tricia scrambled to retrieve them, but when lightning struck a tree on the green, Tricia stared in shock, stumbling and falling over. As a second lightning strike hit The Woolpack chimney,

causing it to collapse, masonry crumbled on top of poor Tricia.

While Louise and Ashley were rescued from their car, with Ashley narrowly avoiding losing a leg, inside the pub, a beam had fallen in the bar, leaving the punters shaken and injured. They evacuated out into the stormy night, seeking shelter at Mill Cottage. 'It was a night shoot, it was very cold when we rushed

out of the pub,' Elizabeth Estensen remembers. 'We were sprayed with water although it was already wet. But you're with friends so you enjoy doing it!' Diane was devastated to see the state of her beloved pub, but it was Marlon who clocked his letter discarded on the ground and was horrified to find Tricia trapped among the debris. As Tricia told Marlon she'd come back to him, a rescue mission was launched, freeing her and airlifting her to hospital, while Marlon, and Tricia's mother, Steph, and grandfather Alan, looked on, desperate for her to pull through.

At the hospital, as Marlon, Turner and Steph waited for news of Tricia, the medics fought to save her life, but her critical condition worsened. Marlon was bereft to learn that Tricia was brain dead and he made the difficult decision to turn off her life-support machine.

The storm episodes had required the expertise of special effects co-ordinator Ian Rowley, now an established hand at *Emmerdale* stunts since the plane crash. 'That was amazing the way they did that: in the dark, with these great big wind fans, and rain on us and all sorts of things,' Deena Payne recalls. 'We had the village set by then, and we wouldn't have been

able to do something like that if we hadn't. It looked great, it felt great, it was great to work on all those night shoots.'

Sugden brothers at war 2002-5

'It was all an act, in front of everybody, while he was stood next to us. That was the happiest day of my life. I didn't think it could get any better. And it was all a lie.'
Andy Sugden

Katie Addyman and Andy Sugden were teenage schoolfriends who, despite her father's disapproval, started dating. When Katie fell pregnant, the teens were desperate to prove themselves capable parents, but sadly never got the chance as Katie miscarried. Nevertheless, Katie and Andy were determined to be together and as they took on the tenancy of Butlers Farm, with Andy keen to continue the Sugden farming tradition, they planned to get married.

For Katie, though, life on the farm was underwhelming, and when Andy's adoptive brother Robert was around, Katie couldn't help but be infatuated. Robert, meanwhile, jealous of Andy's success with Katie and still raw about mum Sarah's death in Andy's fire, set out to ruin the young relationship. 'I think initially Katie wasn't interested, she thought he was a bit of a slimeball, but over time Robert started to persuade and manipulate her that he could give her a more exciting life,' Sammy Winward considers. 'Andy was boring, they lived on a farm, he liked routine, whereas Robert was the rogue, who wanted to travel and do all these exciting things, and he persuaded her it was a more interesting path. But that was Robert wanting what Andy had.'

Katie and Robert began an affair, continuing after she wed Andy. The lovers were almost exposed a few times but, when Andy's brother, Daz Eden, discovered the pair together, Andy refused to believe it and had him sent back to care, while Robert's young sister Victoria became mute when Robert threatened her into silence about seeing him in bed with Katie. 'I think there was a bit of love there, but at the beginning it was about taking away what Andy had, as although Andy was adopted, he was Jack's favourite and Robert was very jealous. He saw an opportunity to get one up on Andy,' Sammy adds. 'He probably didn't expect feelings to grow, but they did in the end.'

As Victoria would only communicate through a very creepy ventriloquist's doll named Alfie, Diane managed to coax the truth out of her, with Jack disgusted at what Robert and Katie had done. Shunned by the family, Katie and Robert tried to make a go of their relationship officially, but vengeful Andy lay in wait for the couple with a shotgun, only to blast Jack by mistake, when he entered the caravan. Jack pulled through, but Katie left the village after her relationship with Robert ended when he had an affair with Sadie King.

Zoe's explosive exit 2005

'I hope Mr King appreciates his housewarming gift.'

Zoe Tate

Having weathered her mental health struggles and the deaths of her father, half-brother and brother, Zoe finally decided to move on from Emmerdale and emigrate to New Zealand with daughter Jean and nephew Joseph. Jean's father, Scott, believed Zoe was wanting reconciliation, and when she turned down his proposal of marriage, he attacked her, trying to rape her. Afraid, Zoe injected Scott with a nearby vial of ketamine in self-defence, but once he was no longer a threat, she made the mistake of injecting him a second time.

Scott made a recovery but Zoe's actions left her facing the prospect of prison on an attempted murder charge. Zoe planned to flee, with nanny-turned-lover Effie Harrison, only to discover Effie had deceived Zoe and revealed her plan to Sadie King. Sadie, now with the upper hand, was keen to get back in the Kings' good books and blackmailed Zoe into returning to Emmerdale and selling Home Farm to Tom King at a reduced price.

On the eve of her planned departure from the Dales, Zoe stood trial, which collapsed after Paddy took to the stand and revealed Scott's intimidation towards him and to Zoe. Zoe prepared to leave, only to have Scott hold her, Joseph, Jean and estate manager Callum, hostage with a shotgun. With the help of Viv and Dawn, Scott was talked down from

rash actions. Zoe left with Jean and Joseph and, passing the Kings on their way into Home Farm, Zoe paused to witness her final act of revenge as, with the help of Callum, she'd timed Home Farm to blow up in a gas explosion.

The explosive exit scenes were filmed on location at Creskeld Hall, which is used for the exterior of Home Farm, and an entire fake frontage was added to the property, protecting it from damage, with false windows and doors blown out. Nick Miles remembers the stunt filming, 'That was quite scary, it was a big explosion. They put me, Charlie (Max King) and Ken (Tom King) in front, then put us out and put the stunt team in to be thrown backwards,' Nick adds. 'It was very exciting, it was a big stunt that won a British Soap Award. I like that kind of stuff, it's very different to two handers and stuff like that.'

Zoe's exit was the last a time a Tate was seen in Emmerdale until 2017, when Joe returned. Following Leah Bracknell's death in 2019, her closing moments in Zoe's spectacular exit remain her lasting legacy to her time in the show.

TIMELINE

SETH'S FINAL RESTING PLACE
2005

Seth had been apart from Betty for some time, taking an extended trip to Australia to see Kathy, but during his long-awaited return trip, Seth died peacefully on the plane. Kathy broke the news to Betty, who was devastated to learn that Seth knew his days were numbered, having been unwell for some time, hence his plan to return home to pass away. Betty planned Seth's funeral and held a wake in The Woolpack, where all the villagers gathered to share their memories of Seth. Betty and Seth's beloved lodger, Biff, made a surprise return to mourn his passing, and Seth's unlikely friend Kim Tate sent a card and

a bottle of whisky in his honour. Uncomfortable with a cremation for Seth, Betty changed the plans at the last minute and arranged for him to be buried in the cemetery, but mourners were confused to find Betty missing. In actual fact, Betty, with help from Laurel, Sam and Zak, had commandeered Seth's coffin and had him buried in his favourite stomping ground: Home Farm woods, where he remains to this day. A duplicate coffin, filled with bags of sand, lies buried in the cemetery.

BELLE AND DAZ'S NEAR-DEATH EXPERIENCE
2005

Christmas was an eventful time for the Dingles when, having been left in the care of drunken Shadrach, young Belle had wandered off with Daz Eden's pet ferret, Spike. Daz went after Belle, who ran off and ended up falling down a mineshaft. Daz tried his best to rescue Belle, but found himself trapped too, with the freezing water levels rising around them. As the family gathered to celebrate Christmas, Zak and Lisa were horrified to find their daughter missing and interrupted the Christmas church service to rally the villagers into a search party. Daz and Belle were found, Daz doing his best to keep Belle afloat to prevent her from freezing or drowning, until they were rescued by the fire service.

The Kings' empire comes tumbling down 2006

'Our girl's gone.'
Bob Hope

King & Sons had expanded into house building, with the show home of their 'Kings River' development complete. However, shunned by the Kings, Sadie had paid Cain Dingle to damage the new house, which he did at the controls of a JCB. The Kings cut corners with repairs, glossing over underlying issues, so the house was ready for a spectacular launch event.

With most of the village present, Noreen Bell sparked a fire in the house when a light in the airing cupboard ignited a gas leak and triggered a series of explosions throughout the house. Jimmy and Sadie, who'd been arguing in the bathroom, were sent crashing through the collapsing floor, while Dawn Woods, Danny Daggert and Diane were all trapped when the living-room ceiling collapsed. Outside, the horrified onlookers could only watch as, slowly, the building collapsed in a heap of rubble.

The party sprang into action to rescue those trapped, with Sadie attempting to finish Jimmy off by smashing his skull with a stone, before she was rescued. 'My abiding memory of that was the director Duncan Foster having me and Patsy Kensit crawling through rubble for two days,' Nick Miles recalls. 'The other thing was they couldn't use a stunt man for the water tank crashing through the ceiling, and they tell you how many gallons of water it is and they say it will knock you to the ground!'

In the aftermath, Noreen, an estate agent called David, and Dawn all lost their lives. 'It was an upsetting thing to do, to imagine your daughter has died,' Tony Audenshaw explains. 'What was particularly cruel about it was that Bob went to see Dawn and you thought she was okay. They had this beautiful heart to heart, and then this awful thing. It was very poignant.'

The Kings covered up the incident, shirking liability, leaving more people with an axe to grind. Tom King's days in the village were numbered...

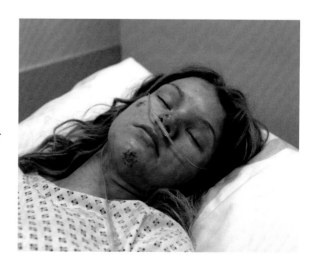

Alice's bittersweet year 2006

'She fell asleep in me arms, looking down at Samson. A few minutes later, she just stopped breathing. That were it, she were gone.'
Sam Dingle

Nice-but-dim Sam Dingle had finally found happiness in the shape of Alice Wilson. But the surprise news of her pregnancy soon turned to devastation as Alice was diagnosed with non-Hodgkin's lymphoma. Encouraged to terminate the pregnancy so she could begin treatment, Alice decided against chemotherapy, instead prioritizing her baby. Sam and Alice welcomed baby Samson in January 2006, but as the premature baby began to find his health, Alice's own deteriorated. Beginning chemotherapy, Alice's attempts to fight the cancer were in vain and she opted to stop treatment.

'It was great working with Ursula Holden-Gill. And it was great to witness the birth of a child, through the show, a young little actor to deal with on set,' James Hooton enthuses. 'Then just the heartbreak of knowing their excitement and joy was short-lived, that this non-Hodgkin's lymphoma story came to the fore, and it was a heart-wrenching story.' Alice began preparing for the future, creating a home for her, Sam and the baby in the flat at Wishing Well Cottage, and marrying Sam in a touching wedding day that included a funfair at the reception. Alice even took part in a sponsored wing walk to raise money for charity.

There was unfortunately no stopping Alice's illness, and as she became bedridden and in pain, Sam struggled to cope. Alice begged Sam to help end her life and he agreed to the euthanasia request, administering a fatal dose of morphine that allowed Alice to peacefully slip away with Sam and Samson by her side.

In the aftermath, the police came looking for Sam, forcing each of the Dingles to admit guilt to protect him, before older brother Cain stepped forward to take the rap. 'It's meat and drink for an actor – particularly a soap actor. You want to be leading a story if you can. With it being an ensemble, everyone gets chance to shine,' James explains. 'For me, that was the first major one. It was great for us to play, to give the full range of emotions, and a joy to be involved in such a poignant story.'

A King's ransom

2006

'You've done nowt but ferry us round the Dales waving that gun about. You're just a petty crook, son.'
Tom King

Cain Dingle and Sadie King had formed a villainous alliance in 2006 and their target was the wealthy King family. Together, Cain and Sadie plotted an elaborate kidnap of head King, Tom, and planned to demand five million pounds for his freedom. Cain kidnapped both Sadie and Tom, and when it didn't take long for the Kings and Dingles to work out the culprit, the great chase was on.

In an exhilarating and ambitious week of episodes, the twists and turns of Cain's plot played out. Cain blew up his trusty old BMW before taking Sadie and Tom, bound up in a stolen car, on a wild police chase. Driving across fields, pursued by police cars and a helicopter, everyone watched on in horror as the car plummeted into the water-filled quarry below. Cain seemingly cornered, it soon proved to be a decoy car, and having escaped the police, Cain took his hostages to a barn. Tom, tired of the games, called shotgun-wielding Cain's bluff, until he shot Sadie in the stomach and killed her. Tom agreed to pay, arranging with son Carl for Cain's sister Chas to make the drop off. Cain met Chas, who left her brother two and a half million pounds, before a fraught goodbye between them and Cain's daughter, Debbie.

Tom was safely recovered by his sons, but with no sign of dead Sadie, it was revealed to be an elaborate hoax when she made contact, safe and sound and with Cain. Reaching an airfield to make their escape by plane, Cain held the trump card as he ditched Sadie in revenge for her paying for Jasmine Thomas to abort his baby. Cain abandoned Sadie on the air strip, making off with the loot, and as he flew over the village, the Dingles watched on, thinking it would be the last they'd see of the family bad boy.

A spectacular 8.7 million viewers tuned into the climax of the story, which had undergone many twists and turns by the writing team. 'They didn't know exactly what was going to happen, just that by the end there was an aeroplane,' writer Karin Young explains. 'So a lot of the structuring I had to do myself, lots of the bones of it, which is sometimes when it's really exciting because you're planning something that's building to something good. I loved Cain and Sadie, and the ending was perfect.'

Who killed Tom King 2006-7

'You've got the wrong one. It's me you should be hitting! It was me, Matt. I killed Dad.'

Carl King

In the aftermath of the Kings' River show home collapse, Tom King's enemies circled, until his Christmas Day wedding to Rosemary Sinclair, when one foe took the ultimate revenge: confronting him in his bedroom, hitting him with a bronze horse statue and sending him tumbling out of the window, to die instantly in front of his wedding guests.

As police investigated his murder, the suspects were many: Tom's sons – Jimmy, Matthew and Carl – had all been threatened with being disinherited, or had their father meddling in their relationships; new wife Rosemary, or her son, Grayson, for financial security; Chas, in revenge for Tom enforcing her break up with Carl; Len Reynolds, in revenge for Tom's blackmail against long-time friend, Edna; and Bob, Terry and Jamie, all out for revenge following Dawn's death in the house collapse.

In a soap first, 'Who Killed Tom King?' was an interactive storyline, with a dedicated online site for fans to turn detective and discover clues. 'It was very gimmicky,' recalls Tony Audenshaw. 'It was like a game to play, and we didn't know what was going on!' Bob was arrested and imprisoned after confessing, believing he was protecting son Jamie, who he thought was responsible. 'It was like *Scooby Doo!* They had us wandering round and bumping into each other, but

we didn't know if we'd killed someone or not,' jokes Tony, 'I remember having a scene with Alex (Jamie), where we both had to act this scene, but we didn't know if we'd done it or not, we didn't know if the other person had done it, and we didn't know if the other one assumed we had or what!'

Lucy Pargeter adds, 'It was really annoying, I like to know the beginning, the middle, the end. It was difficult to film because you'd find yourself doing dialogue but if you had killed him, you'd have played it one way, so it was quite frustrating not knowing how to play lines.'

At the reading of Tom's will, another shock twist was revealed, when the King brothers discovered they had a half-sister, Scarlett Nicholls, the product of Tom's affair with their late mother's nurse, Carrie. As the murder investigation progressed, the King brothers stood accused – their DNA was found on Tom. The Kings faced court, but when Louise Appleton confessed that she and vet Hari Prasad (paid by Rosemary to implicate the Kings) had lied, the case collapsed. The Kings turned on each other, until Carl cracked and revealed he was the culprit.

BEST OF THE REST
2000s

TERRY'S SHOCKS
2003-4

Terry Woods fell in love with Bob's daughter, Dawn, and despite the huge age gap, they got married. Dawn fell pregnant, giving birth to a son, Terry Junior, but while celebrating the birth of his son, Terry had a stroke.

MAX'S ILL-FATED PLAN
2005

Max King tired of his father's manipulation and made plans to leave for London. Catching a lift with Andy Sugden, Max was thrown into Andy and Robert's feud when they embarked on a dangerous game of chicken and Andy's Land Rover hit a wall. Andy escaped but Max died when the car exploded.

NICOLA'S MURDEROUS PLAN
2007-8

Nicola returned, married to elderly millionaire, Donald De Souza, who was in a coma. Disappointed when he recovered, she plotted to kill him and bag his wealth. Donald cottoned on and called Nicola's bluff about pushing him off a cliff to his death. Nicola backed down, humiliated to only receive £20,000 in their divorce.

VIV'S PRISON HELL
2008

In the wake of baby Daniel's death, Viv became an advocate for children's charities. But when the funds went missing, the culprit, Freddie Yorke, framed Viv, who was arrested and sent to prison for fraud when Freddie planted the money on her.

VICTORIA'S GRUESOME DISCOVERY
2008

Victoria, Scarlett, Daz, Aaron and Jake's Christmas Day visit to a frozen lake nearly ended in tragedy when Victoria jealously threw Daz's chain (a gift from Scarlett) onto the lake, and as she

went to retrieve it, Victoria fell through the cracking ice. Trapped in the freezing water, Victoria was saved by quick-thinking Daz, but was traumatized to reveal she'd seen a body, which would later be revealed as Shane Doyle's.

PSYCHO SALLY
2009-10

Vicar's wife Sally Spode developed an obsession with Ashley and tried to eliminate Laurel – first by setting fire to her coat, then by locking Laurel in the burning church. Laurel worked out the truth and left, but as Ashley went to fight for his marriage, Sally threw herself onto Ashley's car. Sally's obsession continued as she trashed Ashley's house, drugged him and tricked him into bed. The reign of terror stopped when Laurel confronted Sally at her flat and dangled her over the balcony. Sally was sectioned.

BIRTHS, MARRIAGES AND DEATHS 2000s

2000s BIRTHS

9 July 2001	**Kirk Daggert**, to Latisha Daggert and Paul Cooke
25 December 2001	**Gabby Thomas**, to Bernice and Ashley Thomas
24 January 2003	**Jean Tate Jnr**, to Zoe Tate and Scott Windsor
19 October 2003	**Terry Junior Woods**, to Dawn and Terry Woods
1 March 2004	**Noah Tate**, to Charity and Chris Tate
6 June 2005	**Sarah Sugden Jnr**, to Debbie Dingle and Andy Sugden
12 January 2006	**Samson Dingle**, to Alice and Sam Dingle
9 February 2007	**Cathy** and **Heathcliffe Hope**, to Viv and Bob Hope
26 August 2007	**Daniel Thomas** and **Arthur Doland**, to Mel and Greg Doland, and to Laurel and Ashley Thomas (but a baby mix-up occurred at the hospital)
22 July 2008	**Harry Hyde**, to Katie Sugden and Grayson Sinclair, with Katie acting as a surrogate for Perdita Hyde-Sinclair
6 August 2009	**Angelica King**, to Nicola De Souza and Jimmy King

BIRTH OF THE DECADE

Viv desperately wanted another baby in 2006, even offering daughter Donna £10,000 to be a surrogate, but just as she thought it was no longer possible, Viv discovered she was pregnant with twins. Bob and Viv had broken down on the moors, in February 2007, when Viv went into labour, with only Viv's ex-lover, vet Paddy Kirk, for assistance. 'I remember sitting in the car, screaming as the waters broke,' Deena Payne recalls. 'Every time there was a contraction, I'd scream. I just thought "let it go girl, let it go!".'

2000s MARRIAGES

24 March 2000	**Emily Wylie** m. **Butch Dingle** on his deathbed
6 December 2000	**Tricia Stokes** m. **Joe Fisher** to help him stay in the country
25 December 2000	**Bernice Blackstock** m. **Ashley Thomas**
5 February 2001	**Viv Windsor** m. **Bob Hope**
27 November 2001	**Charity Dingle** m. **Chris Tate**
2 May 2002	**Gloria Weaver** m. **Eric Pollard**
17 October 2002	**Emily Dingle** m. **Paddy Kirk**
14 February 2003	**Tricia Stokes** m. **Marlon Dingle** after a failed attempt in 2002
18 March 2003	**Dawn Hope** m. **Terry Woods**
17 February 2003	**Katie Addyman** m. **Andy Sugden**
21 September 2004	**Diane Blackstock** m. **Jack Sugden**
6 November 2005	**Laurel Potts** m. **Ashley Thomas**
16 February 2006	**Donna Windsor** m. **Marlon Dingle** **Viv Hope** m. **Bob Hope** (again)
24 March 2006	**Sadie King** m. **Alasdair Sinclair**
24 April 2006	**Alice Wilson** m. **Sam Dingle**
25 December 2006	**Rosemary Sinclair** m. **Tom King**, before he was pushed to his death on the wedding night
19 February 2008	**Jo Stiles** m. **Andy Sugden** in a prison ceremony
3 March 2008	**Paul Lambert** m. **Jonny Foster**
3 June 2008	**Val Lambert** m. **Eric Pollard**
31 March 2009	**Lexi Nicholls** m. **Carl King**

WEDDING OF THE DECADE

2006 saw the wedding of Donna and her mum Viv to Marlon and Bob respectively. In typical soap style, Bob was kidnapped by his first wife, Jean. Viv fled, but was eventually talked round by a returned Bob. After crashing a funeral, they persuaded Ashley to conduct their service.

HENSHALL BURNS THE VILLAGE
2011

DS Nick Henshall began dating Katie Sugden, much to her ex-husband Andy's chagrin, but after she rejected him, Henshall took action by setting fire to Katie's house. Hoping that dashing to her rescue would reconcile them, Henshall hadn't counted on the fire rapidly spreading to other cottages, leaving the neighbours in peril. As the villagers worked to rescue those trapped, Viv, and Terry, who was trying to save her, weren't so lucky and perished in the blaze. In the aftermath, Katie was horrified to discover a similar fate had befallen Henshall's wife, who died in an arson attack. As Katie learned of Henshall's hero syndrome mentality, he pleaded with her to understand his actions. Katie escaped gun-wielding Henshall, leaving him to turn the gun on himself.

JACKSON'S CHOICE
2011

Being in love with Aaron Dingle as he struggled to accept his sexuality was never going to be an easy ride, but builder Jackson Walsh persisted and became Aaron's first boyfriend. After a row, Jackson stormed off in his van and crashed on a railway line. An oncoming train smashed into the wreckage with Jackson trapped inside. He miraculously survived but was devastated to learn he was now quadriplegic. Adapting to his circumstances was tough and despite the best efforts of his mother, Hazel, and Aaron to show Jackson that there was everything to live for, he wanted to end his life. With Jackson pleading with them to help, Hazel looked on as Aaron administered the fatal overdosed drink in an assisted suicide. Despite Jackson's efforts, via pre-recorded videos, to exonerate anyone, Aaron was tried for the killing, but acquitted.

WHO ATTACKED CAIN?
2011–12

Cain was known for his bad-boy ways, but after an affair with Moira Barton, meddling in Charity's relationship with Jai Sharma, and impregnating teenager Amy Wyatt, Cain had more enemies than ever. After unleashing venomous insults to everyone in the pub, Cain was viciously attacked with a crowbar, then left for dead on a dark country lane. Half the village came under suspicion, with John Barton initially arrested, and Cain, having awoken from his coma, pointing the finger at Jai. When it emerged that Zak was responsible, Cain was rocked at the lengths to which his own father had gone in order to teach him a lesson. Guilt took its toll on Zak's mental health, which led to a fraught reconciliation for father and son when Cain rescued Zak from a mental breakdown on the moors.

Indestructible Carl meets his maker 2011

'So you think I'm going to let you walk away from me tonight? Or ever? If you are not mine, then you are no one's.'

Carl King

Emmerdale's 40th anniversary in October 2012 was marked in spectacular fashion, with a live hour-long episode, promising an unexpected death, two births and a wedding. The weddings of Katie and Declan, and Chas and Dan, were both fraught with tension. Megan Macey tried to stop Katie and Declan's out of revenge for Declan stealing all the profits from the Home Fields Music Festival, and resorted to pushing Katie's face into her own wedding cake in humiliation. Meanwhile, Chas and Dan's reception descended into chaos when Chas's half-sister Gennie went into labour on the floor of the B&B, with the baby's father, Nikhil Sharma, assisting in the delivery just before he fainted. While over at Hotten General Hospital, Debbie Dingle gave birth to Jack Sugden Jnr, a saviour sibling for bone marrow to save Debbie and Andy's daughter, Sarah, from her Fanconi anaemia blood disease.

The biggest story by far, though, was the climax of Carl King's blackmail over Chas, who, having just married Dan Spencer, was trying to keep her affair with niece Debbie's boyfriend, Cameron, a secret. Chas had made a risky false promise to flee with

Carl but he caught up with his lying ex. Chas tried to convince Carl she wanted to be with him, but when he forced himself on her, she was unable to keep up the pretence. Fearful that furious Carl was going to rape her, Chas hit him with a brick. Believing she'd killed him, Chas fled. However, as love rival Cameron found injured Carl, the pair argued, with Cameron dealing Carl a final fatal blow.

With *Emmerdale* going live for the first time ever, cast and crew were tense that things would go without a hitch, although not everyone felt as nervous. 'I absolutely loved the live – I doubt that you'll find anyone else that'll say they loved it. The atmosphere was amazing,' Lucy Pargeter laughs. 'Before we walked down to get ready to go live, there was a massive rainbow and we all looked and thought this was either a good omen or going to be horrendous. And I didn't want Tom (Carl) to go, so I joked with him that on the last crane shot pulling out from his dead body, he should just open his eyes! It's live, they can't do anything about it, he wouldn't be dead!'

TOP 50 STORY

Killer Cameron's night of terror 2011

'You killed our Gennie. Do you really think that I'm gonna let you drag Debbie down with this? If you want to shoot me, shoot me, but this is gonna end here and now.'
Zak Dingle

Having killed love rival Carl King the previous year, Cameron Murray then murdered both farmhand Alex Moss and Chas's half-sister, Gennie Walker, to protect his secret. On a stormy night, escaped Cameron returned, wanting to leave with Debbie. Armed with Zak's shotgun, Cameron knocked out Marlon, leaving him for dead in the rapidly flooding pub cellar before Bernice, Diane, Debbie, baby Jack, Zak, Chas, Alicia, Priya, David, Dan, Ruby and Nicola were held hostage. As Zak argued with Cameron and Chas went for him with a stool, the gun went off, with Alicia caught in the crossfire. David begged Cameron to get Alicia help, and he allowed David out with injured Alicia. Alicia pulled through, the event making her and David realize they should be together.

Meanwhile, Debbie talked Cameron round and he released everyone, except her and Chas. Marlon emerged and attacked Cameron, while Cameron pursued Chas and Debbie into the flooded cellar. As the police worked to rescue them, Debbie and Chas escaped, while Cameron, grabbing hold of a live electrical light, was electrocuted to death.

'It was quite intense, I thought Cameron was great,' recalls Elizabeth Estensen. 'It was a whole week's worth of episodes, so it was long hours, but

it was exciting to film, especially in The Woolpack, it was very different to my usual, what I used to call "what can I get you" days!' With many cast involved in the intense week of episodes, filming was a differing experience for the group of actors. 'I remember me and Sam (Bernice) saying it was like we were in a different play: Chas, Debbie and Cameron are doing all this serious stuff fighting for their lives, and then we had us two talking about being hungry and needing the toilet – so we were a snippet of humour,' Nicola Wheeler admits. 'It felt like Shakespeare going on at one end of the room, and a *Carry On* film at the other.' As the finale of the story involved the flooded cellar, a handful of the cast got a taste of Hollywood. 'Me, Dominic, Charley and Mark all went down to Pinewood. They were getting ready to film Hollywood movies so there was Brad Pitt and Johnny Depp, and then *Emmerdale*. There was all of our wagons parked at the side of the water stage, it was like the Clampetts had turned up,' Lucy Pargeter laughs. 'It was amazing learning to dive, we had to go for scuba lessons to learn the equipment. The set was coming apart by the end of the two days and bits were floating around and towards the end you were wondering how much wee was in there!'

TIMELINE

DECLAN & CHARITY'S FATAL ATTRACTION
2013-14

Faced with losing his empire, Declan Macey torched Home Farm. Charity talked him out of suicidal plans and took control, framing Rachel Breckle for the arson, in revenge for her conceiving a child with Charity's husband, Jai. Bound by the cover-up, and a huge insurance claim, Declan and Charity married and became Emmerdale's new power couple. But for Charity, kids weren't part of the plan, so when she found herself pregnant, she had an abortion. Declan's sister Megan put him in the picture about the termination, and he took Charity to a woodland getaway, intent on killing her. As Megan and her son Robbie raced to stop Declan's murderous plan aboard a boat, Declan took aim at

Charity with a flare gun, only for Robbie to intervene and take the full force, killing him. Charity knocked Declan out with an anchor, and he vanished into the water. Presumed dead, Declan made a dramatic return at Robbie's funeral, confessing all about Charity's cover-up of the fire. Declan fled to lead a life on the run, leaving Charity to pay the price for framing Rachel by going to prison.

LAUREL FALLS OFF THE WAGON
2013-15

Following her break-up with Ashley, Laurel grew closer to Marlon and the pair married. But their domestic bliss soon had to weather the traumas of Laurel being carjacked by Ross Barton, leading to a violent confrontation between

the pair, and also the revelation from Marlon's dying ex, Donna, that she'd had his secret child, April, who he would now have to raise following Donna's untimely demise. The stresses took their toll on Laurel, who turned to drink; her secret outed when young April mistakenly drank vodka from Laurel's glass. Laurel spiralled, even getting drunk and passing out while looking after the kids – only April's quick thinking saved Laurel from choking on her own vomit. Even this wasn't enough of a wake-up call, as drunk Laurel accidentally ran over and killed Marlon's beloved dog, Daisy. At rock bottom, Laurel hooked up with a random guy in exchange for alcohol, leaving Laurel with an STI to explain to Marlon. Laurel fought to get sober, but as she made steps to regain her normality, this wouldn't be with Marlon, as they went their separate ways.

Donna's bombshell for Marlon 2014

'You're going to have a lot of fun with your wonderful daddy, who I know will always be there for you. I am so proud of you, April. And I am so happy that I got to be your mummy. Bye my precious girl, live big, love well. And remember, it's all just one big adventure really.'
Donna Windsor-Dingle

Donna Windsor's marriage to Marlon had collapsed by 2009, and she'd left for a new life in Essex, but when she made a return to Emmerdale in 2014, she had more than one secret to spill. Donna was back with a daughter, five-year-old April, who Marlon saved from being run over by a quad bike. Quickly realizing that April was his child, Marlon was stunned and reacted badly to the news. 'It was staggering for him. Genuine upheaval to the point where he was raging about it to begin with,' Mark Charnock recalls. 'And I put his rage down to that he'd missed out on his child's very infant childhood, he felt devastated by that. Originally it looked like he was going to reject April.'

Realizing he needed to step up, Marlon stopped Donna and April leaving in the nick of time, and they moved to the village in a bid for Marlon to get know the daughter he didn't know he had. But Donna had another timebomb – she had a terminal illness. Not wanting to force any kind of bond between Marlon and April, she kept it to herself for as long as possible, but as the cancer grew, Donna was devastated to learn her prognosis was that she had an even shorter amount of time than she'd first thought.

Donna had meanwhile become close to bad boy Ross Barton, who quickly discovered she was a corrupt police officer looking to pocket money to safeguard April's future. The pair helped each other out, particularly when Ross became embroiled with criminal Gary North. When Marlon discovered Donna's memory box for April, he was devastated to discover Donna was dying and helped her film a final goodbye video for April. As Ross and Donna grew closer, their connection with Gary North became deadly, and when he threatened April, Donna set out to get him put behind bars for good. Capturing him, she took him to the top of a car park and pulled him to his death when she jumped off the roof, killing herself too. Ross, Marlon and April were left bereft, and April in particular would struggle for years to come with the premature loss of her mother, ensuring Marlon had to step up. 'Being a dad to those kids, was the making of him,' Mark adds. 'It was a staggering moment, but a life-making moment for Marlon.'

Debbie's deceit comes crashing down 2015

'I chose you, I chose you, I swear.'
'There should never have been a choice.'
Debbie Dingle & Pete Barton

The wedding of Debbie Dingle and Pete Barton was meant to be a joyous occasion, with a lavish reception in the village hall complete with a visiting fairground outside. However, bride Debbie was harbouring a secret – an affair with Pete's brother, Ross. As the newlyweds prepared for their first dance, a recording of Ross and Debbie's admission of their affair was played to the stunned crowd.

At the same time, over at the scrapyard, another couple were coming to blows, as Chrissie White confronted estranged, cheating husband Robert about his blackmail and warped games with her family. Setting fire to his car in anger, what Chrissie hadn't banked on was Adam Barton being asleep in a nearby car and the fire-igniting canisters of propane. While Adam escaped with his life, the pilot of an approaching helicopter wasn't so lucky. Booked by Pete to whisk him and Debbie away from their reception, the pilot struggled to control the damaged helicopter when a gas canister shot into the air and hit the craft. The smoking helicopter crash-landed onto the roof of the village hall, destroying the wedding venue and trapping and injuring the partygoers. 'The moment the gas canister comes up and hits the

helicopter, it was a great shot and we had a massive crane to be nearly as high as the helicopter. It was the same piece of kit that we used for the house collapse,' director Duncan Foster explains. 'The village hall stuff was great, we had a massive cage inside with loads of soft debris in it, so when we open the cages, it looked like the roof had gone in.'

As rescue efforts were underway, Ruby Haswell, trapped and badly cut by falling debris from the helicopter, succumbed to her injuries and died in Dan Spencer and Kerry Wyatt's arms. Meanwhile, Cain stepped up to become a proper father to young Kyle, by risking his own life to coax the terrified kid out of the wreckage, seconds before the helicopter dropped from its precarious position and exploded. 'Huey Quinn, who plays Kyle, was terrified, so my granddaughter came down, she was four, and we rehearsed it and lined up all the shots,' Duncan recalls. 'Huey could see her having a go at it, so he wanted to do it. He went in and he did it, hiding in the cupboard, and then we see Cain rescuing him.'

The huge explosion shattered the mirror maze next to the hall where warring sisters Diane Sugden and Val Pollard had been locked in by their partners,

who wanted them to sort out their differences. Trapped in a tangle of metal and shards of glass, Val allowed Diane to be rescued first, but her selflessness was not rewarded – Val was fatally impaled by a large piece of glass. 'The mirror maze was difficult to shoot because you had to avoid getting cameras in the back of shot,' says Elizabeth Estensen. 'It was a powerful scene because it was hard knowing that Charlie was leaving and that was the end of the character.'

As injured Debbie was whisked to hospital, feuding brothers Pete and Ross came to blows. When Pete seemingly killed his brother during the fight, he panicked and buried him in a shallow grave. Pete would be stunned when Ross emerged several weeks later, reigniting their feud. Meanwhile, as Eric Pollard returned to the village, oblivious to the carnage that had gone on, he was devastated to be told his beloved Valerie was dead. Relieved to be reunited with his wife at their home, he came to realize she was only a ghostly figment of his imagination, who'd come to bid him farewell. 'That was a journey in itself. Exciting,

but with trepidation,' Chris Chittell muses. 'It was beautifully directed. To be working with a ghost, and believing she's there and she's not there, it was quite an interesting few episodes, I enjoyed them.'

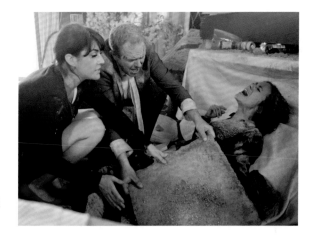

TIMELINE

KATIE'S PLAN BACKFIRES
2014-15

Robert Sugden's return ruffled feathers – now lording it up as he planned to marry into the White family, who had purchased Home Farm, he reignited his feud with Andy, who was reunited with Katie and making plans to remarry. Finding himself attracted to Aaron, Robert began an affair with him, cheating on clueless Chrissie. Katie discovered their illicit love and took photos of them together, confronting Robert on his wedding day. The heated argument turned nasty when Robert pushed Katie, sending her tumbling through rotten floorboards at her and Andy's new farm, killing her instantly. Aaron and Robert covered it up, leaving bereft Andy to find the body and assume it was a tragic accident. Aaron's surrogate dad, Paddy, discovered the affair and Robert took revenge on Paddy's veiled warning to Chrissie, by attempting to kill him

in a grain silo. Vengeful Aaron wanted to get Robert to confess to killing Katie, but this backfired, with Paddy ending up shot. Aaron finally spilled to Chrissie about the affair, leaving her to take revenge that would have huge ramifications for the village.

WHO SHOT ROBERT?
2015

Since his return, Robert Sugden was emerging as the villain of the Dales, and while arguing with Chas, one of his many enemies took a shot at him with a gun. As Robert fought to survive, the suspects emerged: Aaron and Andy were top of the list, and Robert's spurned ex, Chrissie, her son Lachlan and her father Lawrence were also prime suspects – particularly as Lawrence's

gun was used in the shooting. A special rewind episode revealed the much-anticipated true culprit: Ross Barton. Having discussed their hatred of their respective brothers, Ross had made a pact with Andy: to kill each other's brothers, to detract suspicion from themselves. Aaron was arrested for the crime, but as Robert learned Andy was involved he confronted his brother in a deadly game of chicken. Andy crashed his car, and as Robert pulled him from the burning wreckage, the siblings called a truce. Robert fed false information about the culprit to the police, and Aaron was freed. Robert eventually found out Ross was responsible and ensured he confessed in front of his girlfriend, Debbie, who finished with him before she fled the village.

Holly's tragic end 2016

'I don't know who you need to send. It's my daughter, Holly. She's called Holly. She's 25 years old. And she's dead. It's an overdose, I think, there was an empty heroin wrap on the floor. And there's no pulse. And her lips were blue.'

Moira Dingle

Recovering heroin addict Holly Barton had worked through all the traumas of her addiction and finally seemed to be settling down, with a passion for photography and a secret burgeoning romance with Jai Sharma. But one morning, when Moira went to wake her oversleeping daughter, she was horrified to find Holly cold, with an empty drugs wrap nearby. Holly had died in the night.

Utterly bereft, Moira begged her daughter to wake up. Diane Sugden and Chas Dingle called at the farm and found shell-shocked Moira calling the emergency services. Moira's equally stunned son, Adam, arrived to comfort his mother, before going to the pub to lay into Moira's estranged husband, Cain, as the news of the devastating death filtered around the community. 'It was a real, tragic, heartbreaking story, because it just shows that addiction never goes away,' Chris Bisson explains. 'Even though she had all the support, and everything was going well for her, she still made that mistake.'

As Moira prepared to say goodbye to her daughter, she left her with her favourite childhood toy, but as the sadness of seeing Holly's body drive away in a private ambulance became too much, inconsolable Moira collapsed in a despair of tears in the middle of the road, scooped up by a sympathetic Cain. News reached Jai, second-hand, who was devastated to learn of his girlfriend's death. Jai opened up to sister Priya about his romantic connection to Holly, incredulous that she could have given into the temptation of drugs again, when they had so many bright plans for the future. 'He was helping her and they kind of fell in love, it was all hush-hush. It was brief, and that was part of Jai's perpetual bad luck. He'd just found happiness, and they worked well together, on-screen and off-screen,' says Chris. 'People would have doubts and say "you can't put those two together, it's too dangerous!" It was a really heartbreaking story.' Moira, who knew Holly was with someone, gained strength from Jai opening up about how happy Holly was in her last weeks, but Holly's premature death would have a profound and long-lasting effect on Moira.

TIMELINE

BELLE ON THE STREETS
2016

Belle Dingle's attraction to older, married Dr Jermaine Bailey was doomed from the off. When Lachlan White, infatuated with Belle, stirred up trouble by trashing Jermaine and his wife Angie's home, Belle stopped him but was caught by Jermaine and Angie. The affair outed, Angie threw Jermaine out and he lost his job. Faced with losing Jermaine to a new opportunity in Romania, desperate Belle lied that she was pregnant. Jermaine stayed and was reluctantly accepted by the Dingles, but the lie weighed heavily on Belle, whose mental health issues resurfaced as she began having hallucinations in the shape of 'Ellie'. Angie caught Belle talking to 'Ellie' about her pregnancy lie and she exposed the truth to Jermaine and the

Dingles. 'Ellie' encouraged Belle to run away, and she disappeared, sleeping rough on the streets. The Dingles were frantic for missing Belle – Zak and Lisa even having to identify a body. Belle was found and reunited with her family, but it was a long road to recovery as Belle was diagnosed with schizophrenia. Gradually, with specialist care, Belle returned home, and when Jermaine was offered a job in Boston, they parted.

RAKESH'S FINANCIAL WOES
2016–17

Ambitious Rakesh Kotecha's dream of a property fortune turned to a nightmare when his plans to convert Mill Cottage into flats hit expensive snags. With financial woes crippling him, Rakesh took the rash decision to burn down the house for the insurance money – unaware that Nicola King had snuck in to meet Jimmy for some afternoon passion in their old home. As the fire took hold, builder Ronnie Hale braved the flames to rescue Nicola, who'd been knocked unconscious, moments before the building exploded. The accident left Nicola paralyzed on her right-hand side. The feeling in her right leg soon returned, but it would be years before Nicola would regain use of her right arm. Suspicious, the insurance company refused to pay out. Tangled in a web of lies, cover-ups and financial burdens that included getting involved with Chrissie White and trying to frame Andy Sugden for Lawrence's shooting, Rakesh confessed his guilt to the police. Freed on bail, Rakesh made a last attempt to rob the Whites before ditching wife Priya, and heading off on the run.

PADDY & CHAS'S BABY HEARTBREAK
2018

Paddy and Chas's shock and then joy at discovering she was pregnant turned to sadness when they learned that their baby had bilateral renal agenesis, which would mean she might only live for a few minutes after birth, as her organs would fail to develop. Chas and Paddy made the decision to continue with the pregnancy, and as Chas gave birth to baby Grace, she and Paddy imagined the life their little girl would have had, when in reality Grace tragically only lived for 29 minutes.

THE BIG NIGHT OUT TO REMEMBER
2019

On a night out to a club in Hotten, life for some would change forever. Billy Fletcher encountered the brothers of Riley, who Billy had attacked years previously, but after Billy pulled a knife, they targeted his brother, Ellis, and stabbed him. In the aftermath, Billy and Ellis called a truce to their feuding. When Maya Stepney was seen kissing teenager Jacob, Priya, Leyla and Tracy confronted her. Maya jumped from their moving car, but the girls still pushed her to confess to her relationship with Jacob. As Maya gloated about the abuse, Leyla clobbered her with a rock and left her for dead. Maya called upon Jacob's help, as they plotted to run away together.

Victoria was pursued by Lee, who forced himself on her. Victoria locked herself away, before revealing the truth about the rape, and the resulting pregnancy, to her family. Unpunished, Lee hounded the family until Robert whacked him with a shovel, resulting in Lee's death, and Robert's life sentence in prison.

KERRY & AMY'S PLAN BACKFIRES
2019

Having returned to Emmerdale after years away, Amy Wyatt was shocked when Karen, from whom she'd stolen money, demanded her £4,000 back. Kerry suggested stealing a charity collection, but as they pulled off the robbery, they damaged the CCTV system to cover their tracks, accidentally causing a fire at the Sharmas' factory. Frank Clayton turned hero to rescue Tracy from the blaze, but an explosion killed him. His devastated daughters, Tracy and Vanessa, learned of Kerry and Amy's guilt, but their quest for the truth was ruined when Tracy inadvertently injured Kerry, leading to Kerry and Amy's blackmail for mutual silence.

Jacob's grooming ordeal 2018-19

'I tried to tell you both, to get you to understand. Maya's everything to me, but you don't care. It's not an obsession, it's not a phase, and I'm not crazy. I love her.'
Jacob Gallagher

After David and Tracy Metcalfe's marriage collapsed, David began dating Maya Stepney, one of his son Jacob's school teachers, but an illicit attraction grew between Maya and Jacob. Maya groomed Jacob, as they began an affair, even though Jacob was just 15. Maya manipulated and emotionally blackmailed Jacob into keeping their sordid affair secret, encouraging him to take up with his friend, Liv Flaherty, as a cover. Gearing up to have sex with Maya, they held out until Jacob's 16th birthday, when the abuse turned sexual. 'It was a huge responsibility to tell that story with as much authenticity as possible,' Joe-Warren Plant explains. 'It was really the first kind of storyline I'd ever had like that, where we did loads of research, and sat with charities, particularly Barnardo's. We had meetings with kids that had been in those situations in real life.'

Liv discovered Maya and Jacob together and as Maya tried to bully Liv into submission, Liv turned the tables on her, blackmailing her for £10,000. During a girls' night out, Priya saw Maya and Jacob kissing, and she, Leyla and Tracy forced Maya into their car, where she finally admitted to having had sex with Jacob. As Maya made her escape into the woods, Leyla caught up with her and attacked her

with a rock, leaving her for dead. But Maya was alive and got in touch with Jacob, holing up in a hotel with him as they prepared to flee the country. David was devastated to learn the truth about his son's abuse and as Jacob and Maya were tempted back to the village, their cover blown, Maya was arrested, tried and convicted of the inappropriate text messages she sent Jacob, then sentenced to a year in prison.

For Jacob, it was just the beginning of processing things – he lashed out at David and Leyla in particular, struggling to believe Maya's 'love' was grooming and abuse. After Jacob treated friend Leanna Cavanagh coldly after using her for sex, Jacob finally began to realize the damage Maya had done to him mentally and emotionally. Breaking down, he reconciled with Leyla and David and began counselling. 'People came forward to me and said they'd had similar experiences and the storyline had helped them so much. And that is our job as actors, if we can have that connection with one person then we've essentially done our job,' Joe-Warren adds. 'As hard as it was to watch, it helped them in a positive way to express their emotions to people or get in contact with some help. That storyline really meant a lot to me.'

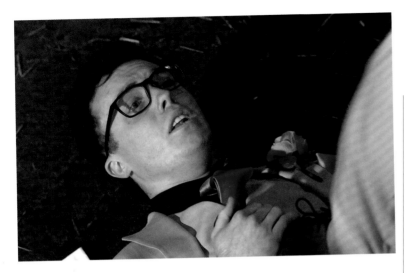

VINNY ENDURES PAUL'S VIOLENT STREAK
2020-21

When Mandy Dingle made a return to Emmerdale she had stepson Vinny in tow, and it wasn't long before they were joined by Vinny's dad, Paul Ashdale. Vinny discovered Paul's weakness for gambling and tried his best to help him, but Paul began violently lashing out at his son. Despite the help of his girlfriend, Liv, and Aaron in trying to get him to face the truth about the abuse, Vinny remained tight-lipped. Liv confronted Paul on the day of his and Mandy's wedding, but they were interrupted when Jimmy King crashed his van into the barn where they were. Unable to rescue venomous Paul, Liv fled, seconds before the barn exploded, killing Paul. Vinny pushed his family away and it was only at Paul's funeral, where he was the only mourner, that he was finally able to begin facing up to the truth about Paul's abuse.

MURDEROUS GAMES FOR PSYCHO MEENA
2021

Manpreet Sharma's sister, Meena, had dumped herself upon the Sharma family in 2020 and soon settled into village life, working at the surgery as a nurse and getting together with David Metcalfe. Meena's strange persona soon reared its head and it was clear she had a dark past, involving the suspicious death of a friend, Nadine. Meena's penchant for collecting strange mementos of her antics hit a snag when the box she kept them in fell into the hands of Leanna Cavanagh.

Meena tracked down her stolen possessions but as Leanna discovered a newspaper article about Nadine's death, she fled for help. On the humpback bridge, Meena confessed all before hauling Leanna over the edge. Hitting her head in the shallow river below, Leanna died. As Meena relished seeing the devastation she'd caused to Leanna's friends and family, her passion for death and deviousness had only just begun.

ABANDONMENT ISSUES FOR CHARLES & ETHAN
2021

Emmerdale welcomed a new face at the church with the arrival of non-stipendiary minister Charles Anderson, who was joined by his lawyer son, Ethan. They were stunned to come face to face with Manpreet, who, under a different identity, had jilted Charles over 15 years previously. The biggest test of the father–son relationship was still to come, when Ethan's absent

TIMELINE

mother, Esme, made contact. Ethan struggled to process that at the time of her disappearance 20 years previously, she'd been suffering from post-natal depression, and that Charles had had an affair. Charles, meanwhile, was rocked to learn that Esme was pregnant at the time of leaving, and that they had a daughter, Naomi.

TRACY STRUGGLES WITH MOTHERHOOD
2021

Tracy Metcalfe was taken aback to discover that she was pregnant by Nate Robinson, but Tracy and Nate planned to make a go of things. Tracy gave birth to a girl, Frankie, who she named after her own dad. Tracy became increasingly obsessed with being the perfect mother, but she kept her worries secret until she disappeared and spent the night sitting in a field. With help from Dr Liam Cavanagh and a crisis team, Tracy was diagnosed with post-natal depression. As Tracy forged ahead with wedding plans, she was gutted to learn Nate had had a one night stand with Fiona – who would turn out to be her sister Vanessa's girlfriend. Nate and Tracy broke up and Tracy seized an opportunity to work for a post-natal depression support group, and moved away with Frankie.

MAIZE MAZE TERROR
2021

Billy, Ellis, Priya and Ben thought they would strike gold with a Survival Challenge, but their plans would turn deadly for volunteers Charity, Mackenzie, Victoria, David, Meena, Andrea, Manpreet and Charles. Angry at Victoria making a play for her man, Meena was incredulous when a rope bridge snapped, sending Victoria, David, Charles and Manpreet plummeting into the rapids below. Although David, Charles and Manpreet all made it out, Victoria went over a waterfall and Meena attempted to finish her off, witnessed by Andrea. Meena taunted Andrea in a giant maze of maize, which quickly ignited when Andrea threatened her with a flare gun. Bashing Andrea's head on the winner's platform, Meena left her to die among the flames. Priya, who was also in the maze at the time of the fire, received agonising third-degree burns to her back.

GABBY GETS THE TATE TREATMENT
2021

Focusing on his relationship with Dawn Taylor, Jamie was irritated to discover Gabby was pregnant after a one-night stand. Gabby found an ally in Kim, who detested the idea of Dawn and Jamie together. Meanwhile, Kim thought she was suffering from dementia as she struggled with fatigue and confusion, but eventually realized someone was lacing her brandy with drugs. Having figured out that son Jamie was the culprit, Kim faked her own death, to shake Jamie to the core. On her return Kim confronted Jamie about his actions, casting him out of Home Farm, while Gabby tried to force Jamie to marry her. As they planned to elope, Gabby was gutted when Jamie crashed his car into a lake and disappeared. Gabby gave birth to baby Thomas, with grandma Diane securing their future by getting Kim to give Gabby a slice of Tate empire. Kim struggled to believe Jamie was dead and he was actually alive and well, hiding out at ex-wife Andrea's mother's house, joined by Millie following Andrea's untimely death.

BIRTHS, MARRIAGES AND DEATHS 2020s

2020s BIRTHS

1 January 2020	**Harry Sugden** was born to Victoria Sugden and Lee Posner
25 February 2021	**Frankie Robinso**n was born to Tracy Metcalfe and Nate Robinson
28 October 2021	**Thomas Tate** was born to Gabby Thomas and Jamie Tate

2020s MARRIAGES

7 April 2020	**Lydia Hart** m. **Sam Dingle**
25 December 2020	**Chas Dingle** m. **Paddy Kirk**
18 June 2021	**Leyla Harding** m. **Liam Cavanagh**
14 February 2022	**Dawn Taylor** m. **Billy Fletcher**
24 February 2022	**Liv Flaherty** m. **Vinny Dingle**

2020s DEATHS

20 January 2020	**Graham Foster**. Beaten to death by Pierce Harris
5 February 2020	**Sandy Thomas**. Died in Australia of natural causes
19 August 2020	**Mark Malone**. Shot dead by Dawn Taylor
28 August 2020	**Annie Sugden**. Passed away in Spain of natural causes
31 March 2021	**Paul Ashdale**. Died of injuries from the barn crash and explosion
7 July 2021	**Leanna Cavanagh**. Pushed off a bridge by Meena Jutla
18 October 2021	**Andrea Tate**. Murdered by Meena Jutla
25 November 2021	**Ben Tucker**. Murdered by Meena Jutla
24 January 2022	**Irene Stocks**. Died of heart problems
4 February 2022	**Pierce Harris**. Died of cancer

WEDDING OF THE DECADE (SO FAR)

Billy Fletcher and Dawn Taylor hoped to put the turmoil of their pasts behind them when they married, but Billy's ex, serial killer Meena Jutla, had other ideas. On the run for her catalogue of crimes, Meena made a return to the Dales, kidnapping Dawn and Billy after their wedding ceremony. Tormenting them with a gun on Hotten Viaduct, Meena revealed she'd hurt Harriet Finch and kidnapped Dawn's young son Lucas. As Meena fled, pausing only to shoot Leyla, Dawn rushed back to the village to rouse injured Harriet, and find Lucas unharmed. Meanwhile Meena came face to face with Liam Cavanagh, who pushed her off the same bridge his daughter Leanna had been killed on. Meena survived and finally faced punishment for her crimes.

CHAPTER 5

BEHIND THE SCENES

'As a team, *Emmerdale*'s an incredibly good storytelling team: the designers, the makeup artists, the camera operators, everyone is a storyteller.'

John Middleton *(Ashley Thomas)*

On a working farm – like that of the Sugdens' at Emmerdale, or Moira's at Butlers – you're up at first light and keep going until the work is done, and that is the mentality of the cast and crew of *Emmerdale*. Offices, corridors, workshops and studios are filled with dedicated cast and crew; every role at *Emmerdale* is an important cog in the overall machine of producing hundreds of hours of material a year. Careers are launched here, whole working lives are spent here, with many staff, on- and off-screen, dedicating 20, 30 or 40 years' service, with cast and crew unanimous that it's a very, very special place to be.

PRODUCING EMMERDALE

'As a producer, I don't see myself in charge of the show, more a custodian of the show for a while, it's a big old ship that's going on a path and you're just steering that rudder to make sure it goes on the right course.'

Laura Shaw *(Producer)*

THE HUGE VESSEL that is *Emmerdale* has the advantage of three captains to guide the soap through successful storytelling. Stalwart of TV production, Jane Hudson, heads up the team, as Executive Producer. Having started a career as a journalist, Jane moved to the script team on *Hollyoaks*, before working on the story and scripts at *Coronation Street*. Becoming the country's youngest producer at 27, Jane produced *Casualty*, then dramas *Robin Hood*, *Waterloo Road* and *Hustle*, as well as *Law & Order*. 'My baby arrived eight weeks early, while we were still shooting *Hustle*,' Jane recalls. 'I remember sitting in the maternity ward with one of the midwives, watching a cut of *Hustle* at about two in the morning, while I was waiting to give birth and she was giving notes on the show!' Jane went on to work as Commissioner at ITV, before landing the role of Executive Producer on *Emmerdale*. Alongside Jane are producers Kate Brooks and Laura Shaw, who share the episode output with alternating blocks. Kate started off her soap career on *Hollyoaks*, as a storyliner, before working at an indie company in Belfast for several years, developing dramas. Kate then worked on the story team at *Coronation Street*, before serving on *Emmerdale* as assistant producer and then producer. Laura has worked at *Emmerdale* for nearly 20 years in a range of roles, working up from archivist, researcher, assistant script editor, script editor, senior script editor,

script producer and then producer. 'I always wanted to work at *Emmerdale*, I was a fan right from being a child,' Laura muses. 'I'm a fan first and foremost.'

Jane, Kate and Laura manage all aspects of the show, both in terms of editorial and production. 'I'm across all story conferences, all scripts, all castings,' Jane says. 'And I work with production so that we're on budget, on schedule, so we achieve everything we want to achieve, can be ambitious and go for big stunts.'

'My role as producer entails a wide variety of jobs that lead to achieving the same goal: how to make *Emmerdale* the best show possible,' Kate adds. 'We start the episode block cycle with a story conference with all the writers and editorial staff. Our job then is to oversee the storylines that are submitted by the story team and carry out story edits.' Once the writer is commissioned and the episode written, the producers are across edits. 'We have several drafts of any one episode before we publish it as a shooting script. I then help oversee the shoot to ensure it all goes as smoothly as possible, before doing viewings on the completed episodes and issuing any final notes in the edit suite,' Kate explains. 'Day-to-day tasks vary, but can involve design meetings, costume meetings, finance meetings, meetings with the cast, as well as any curveballs that may come our way!'

Producing *Emmerdale* naturally comes with huge responsibility, and when dealing with hard-hitting issues and taboo subjects, the producers have to ensure that what goes on-screen is an accurate reflection of real life. 'When we do a story about race and I've got people writing to me saying that for the first time I feel like my voice was told on television, and someone has acknowledged for the first time what it feels like to be this person in this world, when we know we've made a difference, when we've helped somebody, when we've brought somebody back from the edge – you can't get a bigger reward than that,' says Jane.

With a plethora of dramas and soaps easily available to watch, and with *Emmerdale* broadcasting for 50 years and counting, the producers feel the weight of keeping the show current and engaging. 'There's only so many stories that exist in this world: affairs, murders, stunts, children being born. And it's how we tell that story as if it's never been told before, how we make that viewer feel like they've never watched it before,' considers Jane. 'How do we tell a story that's appealing to a 16-year-old and a 96-year-

old, and stories that are inclusive – that include people of colour, people of different sexual orientation, people of different religions? So we've got to reflect the real world and we have got to make sure that everyone feels that *Emmerdale* is part of them, that there's a mirror being held up to their lives, on-screen.'

The producers temper the duty of responsibility with the immense feelings of pride they have for the show, and for the team effort that goes into producing top-quality drama. 'It's reading what our audience say, it's going on the chat forums, which I can't help but do, on social media posts, and I scour them all,' Laura says. 'Yes, you get your negatives, which is fine, we all need constructive criticism, but reading the positive comments of people is rewarding.'

'I've been in this industry for over 20 years and one of the biggest rewards for me is seeing new people come in and watch them grow and flourish,' Jane adds. 'Whether that's someone on-screen or off-screen, and you watch them progress their career and go to the next big thing and the next big thing, that's rewarding to see people go on.'

CREATING EMMERDALE

'Lots of people despise soaps, thinking it's down the other end of life. Reg Watson (creator of *Neighbours*) said to me, "When you've got millions in the audience, there will be at least one person who will see what you've put in, because it's happened to them.'
Bill Lyons *(Writer)*

IT TAKES THE collective efforts of an executive producer, two producers, five storyliners, two story editors, a story producer, a script producer, eight script editors, two researchers, two archivists, seven editorial assistants, and thirty-one scriptwriters to generate around 312 episodes of *Emmerdale* each year. This all starts with a monthly conference, where the first seedlings of an *Emmerdale* story are planted.

'I had no idea that writers on soaps were such a broad range of people,' admits writer Karin Young. 'I thought everyone would be educated, whereas I'd left school with one O level, but I arrived to a fantastic mix.' Karin explains the process of this creative hub. 'Every month, that mix of the detritus of life gets together and we talk about the upcoming month of stories. We argue and toss it all about, and the brilliant thing is, you can say what you want at the table, it's never personal, so some of my closest pals and I can scream at each other about whether so and so would do this, and then you walk out and go to the pub together!'

The story team then takes the ideas to create a grid, episode by episode, categorizing as A, B, C or D stories, of various length within an episode. These are designated to storyliners, who write them up as prose. Once these have been approved by the producers, the story editors compile them as

episodes, before the team commissions writers. 'You get the storylines for the one or occasionally two episodes in the block, and you do your breakdown, which shows exactly, scene by scene, how you're going to create the script. You then write for either two weeks or four weeks depending on where you are in the block,' explains Karin.

The scripts go through a series of edits, overseen by a script editor who also gathers input from the show's archivists, who advise on historical content, and the show's researchers, who liaise with working professionals and charities to advise on factual content. After discussions with the producers and directors, the final shooting scripts are signed off. On a team of nearly 30-plus writers, individuals have different strengths and preferences. 'I would happily do Charity and Chas talking about their toenails for two hours, you could have a lot of stuff starting from that position,' says Karin. 'Any characters with an energy about them are easy to write for – so Charity, Chas, Bernice, Nicola. It's the people who are all rounded really.'

For many budding writers and fans of *Emmerdale*, the key question is how did the writers get into writing for the show? Karin Young trained as a hairdresser when she first left school, before starting training to become a joiner. 'There was a media

course in the building next door,' Karin explains. 'I thought I might do that because they gave you £40 a week and a bus pass!' Karin's reputation as a writer soon developed. 'One of my plays was put on by Vin Welch, Denise Welch's dad, in about 1995, which went down well, and someone who worked on *Corrie* asked for me. They spoke to Mervyn Watson (*Emmerdale* producer), so I did a couple of episodes and Mervyn said, 'Whatever you did with that, keep doing it, you should be fine!'" Karin laughs, 'Like so many creative jobs, it comes from a bunch of coincidences.'

The longest-serving member of the *Emmerdale* writing team is legendary soap opera writer Bill Lyons. 'I was an actor and I did an adaptation of *Mutiny on the Bounty*, and I said "I could write better than this!"' Bill jokes. 'I bought myself a typewriter, it took me three days and I wrote a play. Surprisingly, the BBC bought it. Ron Craddock, who was producing *Z Cars*, was stuck in a traffic jam and he heard it. I wrote an episode of *Z Cars*, and I said, "I enjoyed that, I'd like to do another one" and Tony Holland (script editor and later co-creator of *EastEnders*) said, "that's the first draft Bill, we do notes and drafts." I knew so little about it!' Bill would go on to write for *Crossroads*, *Eldorado* and *EastEnders*, and having first worked briefly on *Emmerdale* in 1984, he returned full time from 1992.

Bill and Karin have penned over 400 and 300 episodes respectively, and across their time on *Emmerdale* they have seen the creative process change. 'When I first started, there was no designated script editor, you had one meeting with the producer to talk through changes,' Karin reveals. 'Now it feels like the machine has got faster – you can be writing one and rewriting two at the same time.'

'The nature of it is it changes massively from being two, to three, to more episodes a week, it eats up story at such a rate,' Bill adds. 'We do character stuff, but we do much less, because character stuff takes time to establish and you need to get inside someone's head. The pace has speeded up immensely, and that's not just *Emmerdale*, that's across television.'

MAKING-UP EMMERDALE

'Continuity is challenging. Anyone new coming into it, it absolutely blows their mind. We probably film 18 scenes a day, on three units, all out of sync, and maybe one artist crossing all those units, so that's challenging.'
Jessica Taylor *(Head of Makeup)*

AT THE HEART of *Emmerdale*'s hair and makeup department is a vast room kitted out with bulb-lit mirrors and all the hair and beauty products imaginable. However, the highly skilled team isn't just responsible for making sure faces don't look shiny on camera, or that there's not a hair out of place; the complex nature of shooting *Emmerdale* demands meticulous planning. Along with a huge output of episodes, a large cast and myriad filming schedules, the hair and makeup team has its work cut out.

Jessica Taylor is at the head of this team and has a wealth of experience in creating the look of some of TV's most recognizable faces. 'I was taken on as a trainee at Granada,' Jessica recalls. 'At that time, they were doing every genre of programme: *Stars in Their Eyes*, *Cracker*, *Coronation Street*, the news, quiz shows, game shows, political programmes, so you cut your teeth on every show going.' Working at *Emmerdale* for eight years, Jessica is no stranger to preparation, as every two weeks she reads all the upcoming scripts, which are then split into three 'units', each with a designated supervisor. Jessica briefs each supervisor on her script notes. 'I'll look for anything in scripts that relates to makeup – somebody's injured, somebody's hot, somebody's sick – all stuff like that we flag up. We'll do a meeting with the director to make sure that everything is how they want it to be.'

One of the most important aspects is continuity. With scenes shot out of chronological order, if a character sustains an injury, it will look different each time they appear, and that needs to be correct for each point in the episodes. 'If a character's got a black eye, we'll have to work out who establishes the black eye on those units: if they were being punched in Unit 1, the chances are we'll be establishing it in Unit 3,' Jessica explains.

Occasionally the makeup team is called upon to create something unique, and that flags up its own challenges, as was the case with the acid-attack story for Ross Barton. 'Ross's burns were the trickiest thing. We really wanted to be truthful to that storyline, but we do have an actor that needed to be made up every morning,' Jessica recalls. 'We simplified it as much as we could. It was like a jigsaw, we got the pieces made and everyone got used to carrying them round in pizza boxes! You could only use them once. It was a challenge but we took a lot of advice from the burns team at Pinderfields. We had a nurse who came in and gave us advice when we first did it.'

Day to day, the makeup teams face an early start as they prep the actors with hair and makeup, ready for shooting their scenes. 'The actors all say the same, it's a nice time of the day for them to get ready,' Jessica muses. 'It's such a small part of the job, but that's when you're like a therapist, they have an hour or whatever in the chair. Quite often the actors running from block to block will be unsure of the scene coming up, so they run through things with us.'

When it comes to shooting scenes, some of the makeup team will be dispatched to the studio floor, checking on the monitors whether actors' hair and makeup looks right, or whether any tweaks or touch-ups are required before takes, to ensure the continuity. 'It's harder in the village, with people's hair moving during a scene – if it blows over the shoulder and in another shot it's back, a director would not be able to cut between the takes that they've got,' Jessica explains. 'And the village gets all weathers, it's very windy up there, so it's quite extreme. It's challenging in the village, trying to keep them all looking good!'

DRESSING EMMERDALE

'If there's something specific in the script, it can be challenging to find the right item. We get lots of requests from viewers, all the time, asking where we bought certain things from.'

Ian Holmes *(Head of Costume)*

MEANDERING THROUGH THE costume store at *Emmerdale* is, on the surface, an unremarkable affair: rails and rails of clothes, boxes of shoes, bags, hats and accessories adorn every available space. Glimpsing a bit closer, even without reading the labels on each section of rail, more recognizable pieces stand out: the dowdy coat of Sam, the designer labels of Kim, the chef's whites of Marlon, the garish shirts of Rodney, the leopard print of Mandy. No item of character clothing is left to chance, every single piece has been planned, measured, bought, altered, laundered and prepared, ready for the actors to wear. Entire wardrobes, from suits or wedding dresses to Christmas jumpers and work uniforms, are all available, all working together to make *Emmerdale*'s characters some of the most recognizable on television.

Organizing and co-ordinating everything costume-based is the job of head of department, Ian Holmes. 'There's about 25 of us – we usually have three units filming, three in prep. So allocated to each of the six units is a supervisor, costume assistant and a dresser, and then we as the costume design office oversee all of the requirements for that unit.' The four assistant costume designers read the upcoming scripts, and together with Ian, break down anything that is relevant or required for characters' wardrobes. Each new item either has to be made from scratch,

or purchased, either online or at a store in Leeds. 'We get the costumes, fit it with the actor and make sure they're okay. We show them to the director, or the producer if needed, and send them downstairs, where we've got the supervisors, costume assistants and the dressers,' Ian explains. 'We'll give the costume to the supervisor allocated to that block, they'll put that on a holding rail, the costume dresser will prep it on the day of filming, and put the costumes in the dressing rooms in advance of the actors coming in. The costume assistant is then on the floor, monitoring all elements of continuity.'

With so many dramatic and action-packed events in *Emmerdale*'s stories, Ian and the team are often called upon for very specific requirements and requests. 'There could be something specific with a character, or there's a wedding coming up, or a funeral, maybe there's a stunt, and we buy costumes accordingly,' says Ian. 'If there's a stunt, we consider how many co-ordinators there will be, and how many repeats of clothing items we need for the performers, and whether there's any health and safety factors with harnesses or fireproofing.'

'When Kim Tate came back we had to have a dress for the masquerade ball for her introduction, so we had to get this right,' Ian recalls. 'Claire King came in a few times and we chatted, then we found a dress sourced locally. The girl who had the store came

in and we fitted it with Claire and there were a few tweaks. It's little things like that, finding something that's a little bit different to what everyone's worn previously and getting that made.'

Whenever the costume team pulls off a unique piece, a costume that proves a talking point on- and off-screen, it's always a moment of pride to see the response. 'We did something on-screen with Mandy Dingle's wedding. We knew the wedding dress would

need to be something that was quite out there, so I was chatting to Lisa Riley about it together and we draw up a couple of designs,' Ian remembers. 'We got inspiration from the internet, that was on *RuPaul's Drag Race*, because the dress The Vivienne wore incorporated some leopard print, so we took inspiration from that. It was quite rewarding to see that.'

DESIGNING EMMERDALE

'Within one day I get to deal with exploding vacuum cleaners, designing prison sets, dressing beautiful weddings where a helicopter becomes an unwelcome guest, and probably my favourite: discussing how to protect reindeer from the rain!'

Gillian Slight *(Head of Design)*

WITH THE QUALITY of television production and broadcasting never sharper, it falls upon the expertise of *Emmerdale*'s in-house design and props teams to ensure 'the look' of the show's sets is top quality. For head of design Gillian Slight, her role at *Emmerdale* is vast. 'My team and myself are responsible for the design and construction of all filming sets, from the initial planning and build stage right through to the decoration, furniture, lamps, pictures and soft furnishings.' One of the biggest departments on the show, Gillian leads a 20-strong team of a supervising art director, graphic designers, buyers, art directors and standby art directors.

When planning a new set, Gillian starts by sitting down with the producers, to get a sense of the requirements. 'I make sure the set suitably reflects the character for whom it is intended. I have to consider the age, income, background and interests of the character in order to create a home or workplace that is right for them.' When planning and executing her vision for a set, Gillian has to ensure she liaises with the lighting, camera and sound departments, to make sure the set works on a logistical level too.

The design team also chooses all the props used on the show and oversees the creation of anything that needs to be specially made, including weapons made from foam, such as Cain's crowbar and the

brick that killed Carl King, to keep it realistic, but also so that it is safe for the actors. 'We also deal with all printed props such as newspapers, magazines, photographs, packaging of fictitious products and all on-screen graphics on tablets and computers, that have to be specially created, like emails, websites, social media pages,' Gillian explains.

'Probably my favourite set would be Home Farm. During my nine years as head of design, it's the set I have changed most often, but the present version is my favourite. It's a large set, designed to maximize the depth, by placing double doors between the spaces,' Gillian explains. 'I can only hope that Home Farm doesn't become a victim of any natural disaster or random arsonist in the near future, which would necessitate a redesign!'

Across a vast yard from the studio spaces is the prop store, the domain of Head of Props, Ian Robertshaw. 'The props store has a team of people working in it; we've got three crews, sometimes more, and they'll come in the morning, collect the props, take them and check them, then they get everything ready for the next day's filming.' Each crew usually has four people: a chargehand, who is in charge of the unit, stand-by props, who have read the scripts and have a little more understanding of the continuity, then there are a couple more people to assist. 'If they're in the studio, they're making food, prepping sets, then going back and cleaning up, to leave it as well as they can for the next crew,' Ian explains. 'On location there tends to be more work, dealing with vehicles and the logistics of being out and about.'

Each character has their own established props within the prop store, which are recorded and catalogued. To maintain continuity and a sense of reality, a character will be seen with the same mobile phone, makeup bag, keys and personal effects. 'The characters that have been there a long time have a lot of stuff,' Ian muses. 'It's just easier to manage that than establish something new all the time, plus viewers get used to seeing the same sort of bag, etc.' With the village exteriors filmed over half an hour's drive away, and with multiple studios to equip, the work of Ian's team is always pressing, 'There's never a dull moment,' Ian laughs. 'The crossovers with props are probably the most challenging for the team; props need to go to the village, with the characters, having been in studio in the morning, so timing that can be quite challenging.'

FILMING EMMERDALE

'With *Emmerdale*, it's all there, you can walk from the café down to the church, you can walk from the church back up to the pub; we can do all those journeys, because they exist.'
Duncan Foster *(Director)*

ONE OF THE BIGGEST, and most important, leaps in the *Emmerdale* production line is shooting the finalized scripts. To achieve this takes the collective, collaborative logistics of an army of crew and staff, either in the production office, down on the studio floor, or on location in the village. Leading any film shoot is a director, and on *Emmerdale* a bank of highly experienced, highly creative directors – both long-established and new, up-and-coming talent – are called upon. Assigned a unit of anywhere between three and six episodes, the director takes responsibility for how their episodes will look on-screen.

One of the most experienced and long-standing directors at *Emmerdale* is Duncan Foster. 'I was an editor, I used to edit a lot of dramas – that's my background really,' Duncan explains. 'I got an 18-week secondment onto *Emmerdale*, I shadowed and then directed a few episodes and that's how I got into soap. I jumped over to *Corrie* for a time, and people could see I could do the gig, so I was off and running.' As with all directors, Duncan's job begins with the scripts. 'It's about our interpretation of what's been written, and then it becomes how we work on the actor's performances, how we film it, will it require a different look, a different narrative to usual, like a Super Soap Week, for example; it's all those sort of decisions,' Duncan explains. 'The director works closely with the producer and we work out how we're

graphics work done, making sure it passes Technical Assessment, and giving our delivery partners enough time to create subtitles and audio description and sign the programmes for our deaf viewers.'

'From a post-production point of view, completing the programme is much easier than it was 30 years ago!' Nigel muses. 'But the fact that we now transmit six episodes a week, rather than the then two, means we are busier than ever.'

CELEBRATING EMMERDALE

'*Emmerdale*, from the very beginning, has always acknowledged the fact that without the viewers, without the fans, they haven't got a programme.'
Jenny Godfrey (*Founder of The Emmerdale Club*)

FIFTY YEARS ON, *Emmerdale* continues to retain a strong audience share for its timeslot, pulling in millions of viewers, six times a week. While fans of the show take all forms, from casual viewers to die-hard 'watched from the first episode' stalwarts, *Emmerdale* is the only soap to have an official, affiliated fan club: a loyal body of fans who have a full calendar of events to celebrate their shared passion for all things *Emmerdale*.

Founded in 1990, the *Emmerdale* Club was the brainchild of viewer Jenny Godfrey, who noticed a gap in the market for *Emmerdale* appreciation. 'I've watched from the beginning, and I loved it. I was visiting an aunt and uncle, who were farmers, and my uncle knew where the farm and village was – in the early days the show didn't disclose the filming locations. My uncle told me where it was, so I went along. I realized that a lot of people were interested,' Jenny explains. 'So I wrote to Stuart Doughty, the producer, and asked if I could start a fan club, but I would only do it with his approval. I had a meeting with him, the head of publicity and Tim Fee, the production controller, and they agreed.'

With a staggering 4,000 members at its peak, the club quickly became an exclusive way for fans to get closer to the show, and the stars, that they loved. 'I thought we can't just let it be one of those things where you pay your fee, get one newsletter, I really

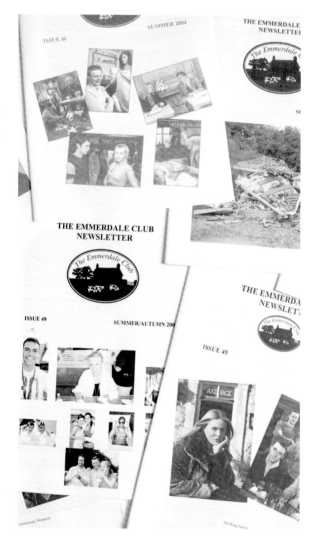

wanted to make it something big,' Tim Fee recalls. 'I was the instigator of the *Emmerdale* weekend, it was massive.'

The *Emmerdale* weekend has become the highlight of the club's year, incorporating a tour of the studios on the Saturday, including talks from crew, and even special stunt displays by co-ordinator Ian Rowley. On the Saturday night, at a local hotel, the club members, along with crew and cast, meet for a gala dinner, and then on the Sunday they head out on a tour of the village set at Harewood. 'The weekends just grew and grew. They became really popular – we have people from Finland, Sweden, Ireland travel over and *Emmerdale* open their doors to us and give us a really fabulous time,' Jenny adds. 'We have newsletters, to keep in touch, and then during the pandemic, Nader (head of production) had the idea of doing online meet-ups, every week, which Alli (PR co-ordinator) has facilitated, which has been wonderful. It's seen some of our members through some tough times. I never anticipated this great friendship, a caring community that has been created, also from the cast. It's a really special thing.'

'I don't think there's another programme of this ilk that has a body of people like this, and they are an integral part of the show,' actor Chris Chittell muses. 'They're like a family that grows and grows, which is a good thing, it's quite exciting.'

FAMOUS FACES

Chef **Aldo Zilli** made an appearance at a cooking competition that Marlon was at in 2005.

Marlon was also thrilled to meet **Antony Worrall Thompson** in 2008, when he was judge of Pub of the Year contest, and auditioned Marlon for a cookery show.

Footballer and presenter **Chris Kamara** clashed with Bear Wolf in 2019, when The Woolpack played against Chris's team in a football match.

Former *Doctor Who* **Colin Baker** made a brief appearance in 2021 as Michael, Diane Sugden's jigsaw puzzle enthusiast date.

Cricketer **Fred Trueman** made a cameo in the Dales in 1987.

James 'Hunter' Crossley of *Gladiators* fame joined the village tug-of-war contest in 1995.

Ian Botham took a break from cricket to act as the celebrity guest performing the opening ceremony of the newly refurbished Woolpack in 1995.

Welsh singer **Katherine Jenkins** performed at Emmerdale's 500th anniversary fete in 2007.

Lionel Blair dropped into *Emmerdale* to judge a dancing contest in 2008.

Wet Wet Wet singer **Marti Pellow** surprised Kathy Glover at her leaving party in 2001.

International rugby player **Martin Offiah** appeared as himself at a rugby match in 1996, organised by Terry Woods.

Spice Girl **Mel B** popped up in *Emmerdale* several times as an extra; first in 1993 at Leeds Station, then the same year in a three-legged drinking race with **Angela Griffin** of *Coronation Street* fame, and finally as an extra, again at Leeds Station, with Rachel Hughes, in 1994.

Olympic boxer **Nicola Adams** worked as an extra on soaps, appearing in scenes in *Emmerdale's* shop and café, as well as The Woolpack.

Presenters **Phillip Schofield** and **Fern Britton** played host to Alan Turner in 2005, as he made an emotional plea for missing partner Shelley Williams to get in touch on *This Morning*. Phillip Schofield made another cameo in 2015 as an extra in the background of the shop.

Richard Whiteley appeared as himself in 2002, interviewing Gloria Pollard.

The Proclaimers and **Scouting for Girls** appeared on stage as themselves in 2012, performing at Declan Macey's Home Fields festival.

The Vivienne appeared as herself to open *Emmerdale's* first Pride event in 2021.

Comedian **Tommy Cannon** appeared in 2019 as Derek, a patient of Manpreet's who died of salmonella.

Tony Booth, father of Cherie Blair, played Errol Michaels, a tramp, in 2007.

Diane attended a concert with singer **Tony Christie** in 2005.

Olympic cyclist **Victoria Pendleton** dropped into Home Farm in 2014 as the celebrity guest at the estate's relaunch.

WHAT HAVE I SEEN THEM IN?

Adam Thomas (Adam Barton)
Waterloo Road

Amy Nuttall (Chloe Atkinson)
Downton Abbey

Chelsea Halfpenny (Amy Wyatt)
Casualty

Chris Bisson (Jai Sharma)
Shameless/East is East

Dean Andrews (Will Taylor)
Life on Mars/Last Tango in Halifax

Gillian Kearney (Emma Barton)
Shameless/Casualty

Jason Merrells (Declan Macey)
Waterloo Road/Cutting Edge

Jenna Coleman (Jasmine Thomas)
Victoria/Doctor Who/The Serpent

Joe Gilgun (Eli Dingle)
Brassic/Misfits/This is England

Kay Purcell (Cynthia Daggert)
Tracy Beaker

Kelli Hollis (Ali Spencer)
Shameless

Linda Thorson (Rosemary King)
The Avengers

Louise Jameson (Sharon Crossthwaite/Mary Goskirk)
Doctor Who/Bergerac/Tenko

Mark Jordon (Daz Spencer)
Heartbeat

Norman Bowler (Frank Tate)
Softly, Softly

Reece Dinsdale (Paul Ashdale)
Threads

Siobhan Finneran (Heather Hutchinson)
Happy Valley/Downton Abbey/Rita, Sue & Bob Too/Benidorm

Stephen McGann (Sean Reynolds)
Call the Midwife

Steve Halliwell (Zak Dingle)
Threads

Susan Cookson (Wendy Posner)
Casualty

Tom Chambers (Clive)
Holby City/Casualty/Waterloo Road

Trudie Goodwin (Georgia Sharma)
The Bill

Alun Lewis (Vic Windsor)
Birds of a Feather

Angela Thorne (Charlotte Verney)
To the Manor Born

Bhasker Patel (Rishi Sharma)
Only Fools and Horses

Bobby Knutt (Albert Dingle)
Benidorm

Duncan Preston (Douglas Potts)
dinnerladies/Victoria Wood: As Seen on TV

Elizabeth Estensen (Diane Sugden)
The Liver Birds

Emily Head (Rebecca White)
The Inbetweeners

Frank Kelly (Dermot Macey)
Father Ted

James Baxter (Jake Doland)
Still Open All Hours

Kathy Staff (Winnie Purvis)
Last of the Summer Wine

Kim Thomson (Faye Lamb)
Brush Strokes

Max Wall (Arthur Braithwaite)
Comedian, and music hall entertainer

Michelle Holmes (Britt Woods)
Goodnight Sweetheart/Rita, Sue & Bob Too

Paul Shane (Solomon Dingle)
Hi-De-Hi

Paula Tilbrook (Betty Eagleton)
Open All Hours

Paula Wilcox (Hilary Potts)
Man About the House

Pauline Quirke (Hazel Rhodes)
Birds of a Feather

Peter Martin (Len Reynolds)
dinnerladies/The Royle Family

Richard Wilson (Mr Hall)
One Foot in the Grave

Shirley Stelfox (Edna Birch)
Keeping Up Appearances/Personal Services

Wendy Craig (Maisie)
Butterflies

Amanda Donohoe (Natasha Wylde)
L.A. Law/Liar Liar

Lesley Manville (Rosemary Kendall)
Secrets & Lies/All or Nothing/Vera Drake/Another Year/High Hopes

Matthew Marsden (Danny Weir)
Helen of Troy/Resident Evil/Transformers

Maxwell Caulfield (Mark Wylde)
Grease 2

Michael Praed (Frank Clayton)
Robin of Sherwood

Noah Huntley (Luke McAllister)
28 Days Later/The Chronicles of Narnia/Snow White and the Huntsman

Patrick Mower (Rodney Blackstock)
Carry On England, Black Beauty, To Catch a Spy

George Sampson (Ryan)
Dancer, who won Britain's Got Talent

Jake Roche (Isaac Nuttall)
Member of band Rixton

Patsy Kensit (Sadie King)
Member of band Eighth Wonder

Suzanne Shaw (Eve Jenson)
Member of band Hear'Say

Lisa Riley (Mandy Dingle)
You've Been Framed presenter

Tim Vincent (Adam Forrester)
Blue Peter presenter

Tracy Brabin (Carol)
Mayor of West Yorkshire

SOAP MOVERS

Adele Silva (Kelly Windsor) – *Hollyoaks* (Angela Brown) & *EastEnders* (Beth)

Alan Rothwell (John Kenyon) – *Coronation Street* (David Barlow) & *Brookside* (Nick Black)

Alex Carter (Jamie Hope) – *Hollyoaks* (Lee Hunter)

Alyson Spiro (Sarah Sugden) – *Brookside* (Alison Gregory)

Amy Walsh (Tracy Metcalfe) – *Hollyoaks* (Jennifique McQueen)

Angela Griffin (Tina) – *Coronation Street* (Fiona Middleton)

Anna Friel (Poppy Bruce) – *Brookside* (Beth Jordache)

Anne Charleston (Lily Butterfield) – *Neighbours* (Madge Bishop)

Anthony Quinlan (Pete Barton) – *Hollyoaks* (Gilly Roach)

Ayden Callaghan (Miles De Souza) – *Hollyoaks* (Joe Roscoe)

Ben Freeman (Scott Windsor) – *EastEnders* (Caleb Malone)

Beverley Callard (Angie Richards) – *Coronation Street* (Liz McDonald)

Bill Ward (James Barton) – *Coronation Street* (Charlie Stubbs)

Catherine Tyldesley (Abi Peterson) – *Coronation Street* (Eva Price)

Chris Bisson (Jai Sharma) – *Coronation Street* (Vikram Desai)

Claire King (Kim Tate) – *Coronation Street* (Erica Holroyd) & *Hollyoaks* (prison governor)

Craig Fairbrass (Gypsy Man) – *EastEnders* (Dan Sullivan)

Craig Vye (Dean) – *Hollyoaks* (Ethan Scott)

Daniel Brocklebank (Ivan Jones) – *Coronation Street* (Billy Mayhew)

David Easter (Gil Keane) – *Brookside* (Pat Hancock) & *Hollyoaks* (Mac Nightingale)

Denise Black (Joanie Wright) – *Coronation Street* (Denise Osborne)

Diana Davies (Caroline Bates) – *Coronation Street* (Norma Ford)

Dicken Ashworth (Duke Woods) – *Coronation Street* (Geoff Horton) & *Brookside* (Alan Partridge)

Elizabeth Estensen (Diane Sugden) – *Coronation Street* (Pam Middleton)

Emily Symons (Louise Appleton) – *Home and Away* (Marilyn Chambers-Fisher)

Fred Feast (Martin) – *Coronation Street* (Fred Gee)

Gaynor Faye (Megan Macey) – *Coronation Street* (Judy Mallett)

Gemma Atkinson (Carly Hope) – *Hollyoaks* (Lisa Hunter)

Gillian Kearney (Emma Barton) – *Brookside* (Debbie McGrath)

Glynis Barber (Grace Barraclough) – *EastEnders* (Glenda Mitchell)

Graeme Hawley (Martin Crowe) – *Coronation Street* (John Stape)

Hayley Tamaddon (Delilah Dingle) – *Coronation Street* (Andrea Beckett)

Helen Pearson (Carol Wareing) – *Hollyoaks* (Frankie Osborne)

Ian Kelsey (Dave Glover) – *Coronation Street* (Vinny Ashford)

Jacqueline Pirie (Tina Dingle) – *Coronation Street* (Linda Sykes)

James Sutton (Ryan Lamb) – *Hollyoaks* (John Paul McQueen)

Jane Cox (Lisa Dingle) – *Coronation Street* (Mrs Shaw) & *Brookside* (counsellor)

Jennie McAlpine (Michelle) – *Coronation Street* (Fiz Stape)

Jim Millea (Pete Whiteley) – *Hollyoaks* (Neville Ashworth)

Joe Gilgun (Eli Dingle) – *Coronation Street* (Jamie Armstrong)

John Bowe (Lawrence White) – *Coronation Street* (Duggie Ferguson)

John McArdle (Ronnie Hale) – *Brookside* (Billy Corkhill)

John Middleton (Ashley Thomas) – *Coronation Street* (John Hargreaves & hospital consultant)

Johnny Leeze (Ned Glover) – *Coronation Street* (Harry Clayton)

Jonathan Wrather (Pierce Harris) – *Coronation Street* (Joe Carter)

ACKNOWLEDGEMENTS

This book could not have happened without the support, guidance and input of the following people and I am extremely grateful for the contribution of every one:

Those who provided invaluable interview content: Deena Payne, Frazer Hines, Freddie Pyne, Ian Sharrock, Jean Rogers, John Middleton, Malandra Burrows, Peter Amory, Sammy Winward, Charlotte Bellamy, Chris Bisson, Chris Chittell, Claire King, Eden Taylor-Draper, Isabel Hodgins, James Hooton, Joe-Warren Plant, Jurell Carter, Lisa Riley, Liz Estensen, Lucy Pargeter, Mark Charnock, Michelle Hardwick, Nick Miles, Nicola Wheeler, Samantha Giles, Tony Audenshaw, Bill Lyons, Duncan Foster, Gilly Slight, Ian Holmes, Ian Robertshaw, Ian Rowley, Jane Hudson, Jenny Godfrey, Jessica Taylor, Karin Young, Kate Brooks, Laura Shaw, Mike Laffan, Nader Mabadi, Nigel Duckett, Paul Laffan, Tim Fee.

Those who provided additional assistance and logistics: Ezra Tren-Humphries, Clare Golds, Estelle Hind, Clare Cooper-Marshall, David Crook, Amanda-Jane Dean, Abigail Kemp, Rowley SFX, The Laffan family: Jeanne, Mike, Paul & Dave, the *Emmerdale* Club, in particular Jenny Godfrey, Paul Dacombe and Steve Marshall, Joanna Wilcock, Lee Pickering, Sue Parker, Jessica Foy, Jenny Hamilton, Chris Joslin, Alli Piggott, and to Holly Foster for being a keen and invaluable sounding board for all things *Emmerdale*.

Those involved in the production and publishing of the book: Richard Clatworthy, Jeff Parker at jeffparkerart. co.uk, and everyone at Octopus Publishing, especially Juliette Norsworthy, Pauline Bache and Trevor Davies.

Particular thanks go to John Whiston and Jane Hudson, to Laura Shaw for all of your continued motivation, mentoring and advice, and Shirley Patton for your shared enthusiasm in facilitating this book from the very beginning.

Lastly, many thanks to my family and friends, in particular Maddie, Ruth, Mari and Chris, Lorna, and David, Jeff and Frances, for your endless support and encouragement.